STOP WASTING TIME

STOP
WASTING
TIME

End Procrastination
in 5 Weeks with Proven
Productivity Techniques

Garland Coulson

**ALTHEA
PRESS**

Interior and Cover Designer: Jamison Spittler
Editor: Camille Hayes
Production Editor: Erum Khan

ISBN: Print 978-1-64152-145-1 | eBook 978-1-64152-146-8

CONTENTS

HOW TO USE THIS BOOK

Why a Five-Week Program?

Let's be honest. This probably isn't the first book you've read on productivity or procrastination. That's okay—I'm not offended that I'm not your first. The truth is that all of us, even the most successful, are interested in learning how to be more productive.

You've probably read a lot of books with great-sounding ideas that never resulted in the productivity breakthroughs you were looking for. That is why, instead of writing another ineffective book that will just sit on your shelf collecting dust, I developed a five-week program that you can actually implement and follow through on. Instead of just talking about how you *could* improve, this guide provides clear, step-by-step instructions to *stop wasting time*.

So, what business do I have writing about procrastination and why should you take my advice? These days, I work as a time management consultant, but I haven't always been an expert on these matters. My time management journey started in my early twenties when I worked in a busy banking environment. I was a young, gung ho, low-level manager, fairly competent and hard-working but with mediocre time management skills. My time management wasn't so poor that it kept me from getting the job done, but my inability to make the most of my working hours prevented me from excelling.

Then, one Christmas, my manager gave me a lovely red leather day planner as a gift. As I assembled the pages in the binder, I was blown away by the brilliance and elegance of the planning system. In addition to a daily calendar with appointment slots, the calendar pages also had space for keeping track of calls to make, expenses, and tasks. There were even entire sections dedicated to goal-setting, client notes, meeting notes, and more. The level of organization this simple tool provided me was astounding, and it opened my mind to a whole new level of thinking about how I worked and how I organized my time.

From that moment, I was hooked. I became obsessed with learning about time management, and I voraciously devoured every book, article, and training program I could find on the subject. I listened to audio courses on time management in my car while commuting to work every day. I started helping my colleagues get organized and showed them how to use their time more effectively.

As my understanding deepened, my colleagues started coming to me for advice, and I eventually learned the lesson many other "masters" do: To truly understand something, you have to teach it. Teaching a topic requires breaking it down and distilling it into its purest, most powerful form so that you can help others understand the topic clearly and master it efficiently. I found that teaching others helped me incorporate the principles of time management into my life even faster. I soon began running in-house training workshops for companies I worked for and eventually started my own business teaching time management. Now I speak in front of and train thousands of people each year, and I'm proud to say that I am affectionately known to my students and clients as Captain Time.

The techniques and strategies in this book aren't just things I've made up to sound catchy or seem clever. They are drawn from cutting-edge thinking in mindfulness practices and psychology. Everything I recommend here has been tested by researchers and proven to work. Further, I have personally tested and proven many of these techniques on my willing students and clients. Thousands of people have benefitted from these strategies, and their experiences have helped me refine how I use them.

Think of this five-week program as your own personal time management GPS. Your destination is a procrastination-free lifestyle, and I'm going to give you the step-by-step driving directions to reach this goal. You will need to partner with me on this. The program won't magically "cure" you if you don't put in the work. But the beauty of this program is that there's not much to figure out—I will tell you what to do and when to do it, and your main job will be setting aside time in your schedule to work on the program.

To find success, you'll need about 20 minutes a day to complete the exercises and action steps included in the program. This may sound like a lot, but this time will largely be spent making to-do lists and building your daily schedule—productive work you already need to do. This daily time investment will pay off, as it will save you much more than 20 minutes a day once you have your new productivity strategies in place and are using them as a regular part of your routine.

By the time you've completed this program, you will:

➤ Understand why you procrastinate

➤ Learn techniques to stop procrastinating

➤ Build a "superstructure" around your schedule to make sure all your tasks get completed

➤ Learn to focus your attention where it needs to be to maximize results

➤ Implement a self-motivation program

➤ Build the foundation for lifetime success

An important feature of this program is that it can be customized to suit your specific needs. My years of coaching have taught me that there is no one technique or tool that works for *every* client. Instead, I learn about each client's challenges and productivity approach and customize my coaching accordingly. This five-week program allows you to do the same regarding your personal productivity. As you work through the steps, you will be able to identify and implement the techniques that work best in your own case—the techniques that help you reach your goals.

Throughout this book, I will mention tools and apps you can use to get organized. These were my favorite productivity tools at the time I wrote this book. Of course, new tools come out often, so my favorite tools may change. You can see the latest tools I am using to solve productivity problems on the "Tools" page of my website at CaptainTime.com, or you can e-mail me at garland@captaintime.com.

Working the Five-Week Program

Prior to beginning the program, I want you to get a small lined notebook to write in. We'll call it your "Stop Wasting Time" notebook. If you already have a day planner, you can keep that handy as well, but most of the work will be completed in your notebook. If you want to choose a decorative or leather notebook, go ahead, but a simple dollar-store notebook will work as well. Don't procrastinate—find or purchase your notebook now. It's a simple first step, but the notebook will be an important tool throughout the program.

In addition to your notebook, you'll also need to set aside 20 minutes daily to do the recommended exercises and planning. Make a commitment to invest in yourself, and keep this time sacred! Don't let *anything* or *anyone* take your 20 minutes of planning time away. Block it off on your calendar, highlight it in yellow, and let your friends and family know that time is for you. Committing to this time is an important step on your road to success.

This five-week program has no fluff or filler; it's designed for maximum efficiency. If you stay focused and work the program persistently every day, by the end you will have the mental and organizational skills you need to break your procrastination habit for good. What will that mean for you? It will mean better organization, less stress, and more success at work and in your personal life.

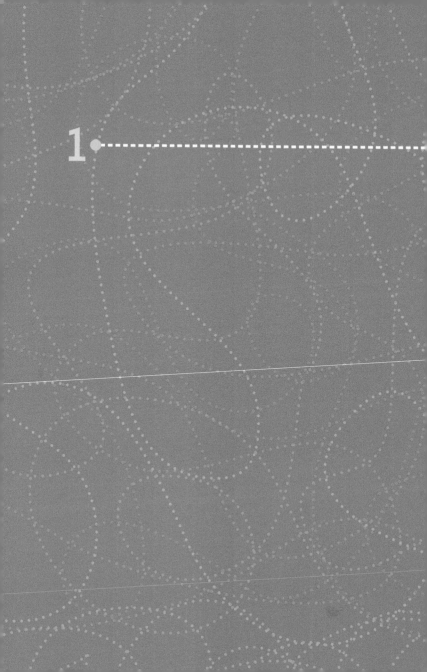

1

What's Holding You Back?

Why Do We Procrastinate?

Over the course of this five-week program, I'm going to help you get to the root of your procrastination and give you powerful, effective strategies to solve the underlying problems that trigger it instead of just masking your symptoms with motivational buzzwords.

This book is in your hands because you are at a point in your life where you realize that procrastination is causing serious problems for you. Perhaps missed deadlines at work are adding to your stress or even jeopardizing your job. You might be frustrated that you can't make any meaningful progress toward your professional or personal goals. Maybe waiting too long to take care of things at home is hurting your family relationships or your financial health.

Whatever the reason, procrastination can be crippling to our career and home life. So why do we procrastinate despite all the problems it causes? Why are procrastinators willing to keep paying the price? When I'm coaching clients on overcoming procrastination, I always start with the "why." *Why* do you procrastinate? In most cases, procrastination isn't the result of not having enough time; it's the result of making time-related choices that allow us to avoid the tasks we're putting off.

So to break yourself of your procrastination habit, you need to understand why you are choosing to focus on other things instead of the tasks you really need to get done. In other words, you need to understand what your payoff is for continuing to procrastinate. What are you getting out of it? The downsides of procrastination are clear, but what are its benefits?

Trying to fix procrastination without first understanding why you procrastinate is like trying to solve a leaky roof by placing a bucket on the floor to catch the water when it rains. Yes, you're preventing damage to your carpet in the short term, but until you know *why* the roof is leaking and address the root of the problem, the leak will return with the next rainstorm. By dealing with the root problem (the hole in your roof) instead of the symptoms (water on the floor), you can fix the real problem, permanently. So too with procrastination: When you know the reason you procrastinate, you can fix the root problem.

Generally speaking, when people procrastinate, they are avoiding some kind of unpleasant internal experience (i.e., thoughts or emotions) that the task they're putting off triggers in them. To take a very common example, pretend you have to give a presentation at work or school. If the presentation is on a topic you are familiar with, then prepping for it should be no big deal since you know the material so well. Yet the days slip by, and you find yourself putting off preparation until you're backed into a corner: The presentation is the next day, and you haven't even started putting together your material.

Since actually preparing for the presentation shouldn't be difficult, what exactly is your procrastination getting you? Chances are, your procrastination is being rewarded by the temporary relief you feel when you avoid thinking about being watched or judged by your audience. Every day you put off preparing for that presentation is another day you get to avoid feeling the anxiety that situation causes you.

Here are some other examples of tasks and the unpleasant emotions they can trigger, which can cause people to avoid them, resulting in procrastination:

Tedious or uninteresting tasks: These can bring up feelings of boredom or indifference—for example, an office person might find it boring to be doing the bookkeeping entries and gravitate toward more interesting tasks instead.

Long-term tasks with poorly defined end dates: Quick, well-defined tasks give us the immediate gratification of completion, but long, difficult tasks can bring up feelings of frustration and uncertainty.

Tasks one lacks skills in: It's more comfortable to do things that are familiar than to learn new skills, as this can bring up feelings of inadequacy and requires a lot of effort to get past it.

Unpleasant tasks: Doing something we find unpleasant can make us feel resentful and frustrated. For example, I once had to write a business plan for a client's product that I couldn't mentally connect with, which made my task unpleasant and difficult. (I set up a strategy to stop avoiding the task despite my discomfort and finished the business plan two weeks early.)

Tasks associated with conflict: Nothing is more emotionally draining than being in conflict situations. It's natural to want to put them off, hoping the problem will somehow resolve itself. But that tactic never works in the long term, and in the short term, it can create even more problems.

Tasks delegated by an individual/employer you dislike: It's difficult to execute projects in a timely fashion when a person feels angry or resentful toward their manager, coworkers, or the workplace in general. Feeling angry interferes with the motivation to get things done and can cause feelings of indifference about tasks.

Overwhelming tasks: The task ahead may feel like too much to handle because there are many parts involved in seeing it through to completion. For example, a long list of household chores like vacuuming, mopping the floor, dusting, cleaning out the fridge, washing the linens, and so on seems so huge that you feel overwhelmed just thinking about it.

Most of my clients are successful in most areas of their lives. They're brilliant, creative, and hardworking, but they all struggle with procrastination to the extent that they have sought my help. Why are brilliant, hardworking people still struggling with procrastination—a problem that seems like it should be easy, or at least straight-forward, to solve? Underlying all my clients' avoidance is usually some sort of emotional or psychological response that's preventing them from living up to their full potential.

Emotional reactions creep up on you, and they can quickly cause you to self-sabotage your work, your personal goals, and your relationships. And, as anyone who has ever been in a heated argument knows, logic rarely makes any headway against an emotional reac-tion. At work, we're taught that we are supposed to be all businesslike and professional, so we tend to stuff our emotions down and ignore them. But even tasks at home, like cleaning out the garage or fixing that leaky roof, can have emotional components that interfere with productivity.

Let's turn now to some quick descriptions of the most common types of procrastinators so you can see which profile best describes you.

What Kind of Procrastinator Are You?

In my more than 20 years of teaching time management, I've found that most procrastinators fit into a few basic categories. By understanding which category best describes your own case, you can identify the techniques that work best for your type of procrastination.

Below is a sketch of each of the basic procrastination "types." You've likely fallen into more than one category at some point in your life, but try to identify the type that most resonates with why you are procrastinating now.

The Worrier

The Worrier focuses on things that could go wrong and is fearful they won't finish on time or do a good job. The Worrier spends massive amounts of mental energy on these imagined problems. This leaves them no energy left to complete the task.

I spend so much time stressing about deadlines and imagining what will go wrong that I get behind.

The Worrier thinks they are working hard on the task because they are spending so much mental energy *thinking* about the task, but they don't realize that all that time spent worrying doesn't bring them even one minute closer to completion of the task. It actually makes things worse because the worrying keeps them from doing the task and can result in negative consequences when the task isn't complete. So the Worrier triggers even more dire consequences by being worry-focused instead of task-focused.

Are you a Worrier? Ask yourself these questions to see:

➤ Am I spending a lot of time thinking about the task before I finally sit down and start it?

➤ Do I have trouble sleeping at night because the things that need to get done are weighing on my mind?

➤ Do I feel exhausted by the task before I've even started it?

If your answer is yes to one or more of these questions, you might be a Worrier. Over the five-week program, you will learn how to harness your worry-focused energy and turn it into task-focused energy to get more done.

The Perfectionist

The Perfectionist needs each project to be "perfect," so they spend their time continually revising the task or endeavor in an attempt to make it better—

I spend so much time revising and looking for mistakes that I never finish.

and as a consequence, they can never let anything go. This can cause a single project or goal to tie up all their time, while other critical projects and tasks remain unfinished because they are spending too much time on the first one.

Perfectionists can become paralyzed by the fear of not executing the project perfectly. They can spend a lot of time spinning their wheels, over-planning, trying to account for all the unknown variables, and doing unnecessary revisions. Since we can never know everything or account for every variable, and the world will never be perfect, the Perfectionist's approach leaves them in an endless cycle of incompletion.

Are you a Perfectionist? Ask yourself these questions to see:

➤ Am I obsessed with having a flawless outcome when I perform a task, reviewing it over and over again to make sure there are no mistakes?

➤ Do I only like to do tasks I am good at?

➤ Does constructive criticism feel like an attack?

If your answer is yes to one or more of these questions, you might be a Perfectionist. With this five-week program, you will learn techniques to finish tasks to an acceptable standard without overcommitting to a single task and leaving other important items undone.

The People Pleaser

The People Pleaser just wants to help! So they say yes to every request without assessing how it will affect their schedule. As they take on more and more work and personal requests from other people, their own tasks get pushed to the side. They become overloaded, but they just can't seem to say no.

At work, as People Pleasers take on more and more, their core workload that they are being paid for and evaluated on begins to suffer, putting their jobs and careers in jeopardy. At home, they often find themselves exhausted by the end of the day without having completed what they personally wanted or needed to do.

Are you a People Pleaser? Ask yourself these questions to see:

- ➤ Am I always the first to volunteer to help out or take on more work?
- ➤ Do I have difficulty saying no when someone asks me to help or to join in an activity I don't really enjoy?
- ➤ Do I work more hours a week than I am paid for?

If your answer is yes to one or more of these questions, you might be a People Pleaser. This program will teach you how to properly evaluate priorities and the items on your schedule so you don't fall into the trap of taking on more than you can handle.

The Hummingbird

The Hummingbird flits from task to task. They feel busy, but very few long-term projects get completed. They are often easily bored or frustrated. They are multitaskers, working on lots of small tasks, but are never really able to take on the larger tasks that require deeper focus and sustained attention.

> I jump around from project to project. I'm busy all day, but nothing ever gets finished.

Hummingbirds often gravitate to small jobs they can complete quickly, which gives them immediate gratification. This causes problems for them when the larger projects and tasks come due and are lagging.

Are you a Hummingbird? Ask yourself these questions to see:

- Do I work all day on many tasks, but never get the larger or more important tasks done?
- Is it hard for me to listen or sit still in meetings?
- Do I regularly start new hobbies and drop them quickly or jump from task to task without completing the first one?

If your answer is yes to one or more of these questions, you might be a Hummingbird. You can use the five-week program to reduce multitasking, improve focus, and accomplish deeper, more meaningful work.

The Closet Procrastinator

Most people won't notice a Closet Procrastinator in action because they aren't missing any deadlines. But the only reason they're meeting these deadlines is because they put in a Herculean last-minute effort to make it work.

The Closet Procrastinator is under continual stress, turning in lower-quality work and courting burnout with their eleventh-hour heroics.

I always get my tasks done on time, but I put everything off for so long that I exhaust myself doing it.

The Closet Procrastinator tries to justify this approach by claiming, "I work best under pressure." But this isn't really true. They aren't delivering their best work; rather, they are delivering some hastily put together work that the deadline forced them to finish at the last minute. The quality of this level of work is typically lower than it would have been if they'd allowed themselves more time to work.

Because Closet Procrastinators are doing things at the last minute, they also lose the ability to consult with colleagues or family members, and research better approaches or alternatives. When given time to work on a problem, your unconscious mind works like a mental back burner, simmering away on the problem and "cooking up" solutions you may not have thought of.

Are you a Closet Procrastinator? Ask yourself these questions to see:

> Do I prefer to work under pressure?
> Do I wait too long to book time-sensitive things like concert tickets or vacation travel?
> Do I work late to meet a deadline because I waited until the last minute to get it done?

If your answer is yes to one or more of these questions, you might be a Closet Procrastinator. The five-week program will help you complete tasks well before they need to be completed while still having time for changes, research, and thought, which will improve the quality of your end product and eradicate the high stress that last-minute execution causes.

Find Your Procrastination Patterns

Now that you have at least some sense of which type (or types) of procrastinator you are, take a moment to do a couple of quick self-assessments to help you identify your personal procrastination patterns. What type of tasks do you avoid? What type of emotions come up for you when you are faced with these tasks? This information will help you strategize as you work through the program.

Self-Assessment: Types of Tasks

In your Stop Wasting Time notebook, title a new page "Tasks I Procrastinate On." Draw lines down the page to make four columns; label the columns "Task," "Procrastination Level," "Stress Level," and "Category." (See the example on page 14.) You can also use a simple spreadsheet or table in your word-processing software, but print it out and keep it with your notebook so that all your notes are in one place.

Start filling out this table by looking at your to-do list. What tasks have been on your to-do list for a long time? If you don't have a to-do list, you can analyze each task as it comes up during your day.

Record the task in the first column. In the next column, rate your stress level from 1 to 5, depending on how stressed the task makes you feel (1 is little or no stress and 5 is extreme stress). In the third column, use the same ranking from 1 to 5 for how often you procrastinate on these tasks. Then, in the last column, add one of the following categories or think of your own:

- Challenging
- Easy
- Large
- Vague deadline
- Open ended
- Group project
- Solo project
- Detail task
- Task outside my skill set
- Task from certain people

This assessment is a self-diagnostic tool because it helps you spot trends. Perhaps you do great with solo tasks but struggle with group projects. Or you might work great when you have a firm deadline but never seem to get going on open-ended projects or projects with a vague end date. Knowing which types of tasks create problems for you helps you figure out the best strategies to deal with them to prevent procrastination in future.

TYPES OF TASKS: SAMPLE WORKSHEET

TASK	STRESS LEVEL	PROCRASTINATION LEVEL	CATEGORY
Answer e-mails	1	1	Detail
Phone irate client	4	3	Challenging
Write marketing plan	2	5	Open ended
New product development group	2	5	Open ended
Vacuum	1	1	Easy
Paint house	2	5	Large
Discuss a serious personal issue with a family member	4	3	Challenging

In this example, this person is not procrastinating when it comes to answering e-mails. They procrastinate somewhat only when having to do something stressful and challenging, like calling an irate client or discussing a serious personal issue with a family member. Their procrastination kicks in at the highest level when they have a large, open-ended project (like writing a marketing plan) or when working on a group project or planning to paint their entire house. Another person may have no problem with open-ended projects but will put off conflict-related tasks.

Understanding the types of tasks you procrastinate on helps you tailor your action plans to stop procrastinating. Understanding the feelings that come up for you when you think about each task takes your plan to the next level.

Self-Assessment: Feelings about Tasks

In your Stop Wasting Time notebook, title a new page "Feelings." On this page, write down all the feelings you notice in yourself when you avoid tasks or take steps toward a goal with a high procrastination level. You can refer to the list of tasks you compiled in the previous self-assessment. Being aware of your feelings and why you are avoiding them is powerful knowledge that will aid in your effort to stop wasting time and get things done.

You can choose feelings from the following feelings list and include anything you're feeling that's not listed:

FEELINGS	
Afraid/fearful/scared/worried	Aggravated/annoyed/exasperated
Ambivalent/indifferent/bored	Angry/bitter
Anxious	Awkward
Confused/uncertain	Disappointed/dismayed
Distrusting/disturbed	Frustrated/irritated
Helpless/powerless	Hesitant
Hopeless	Insecure/self-conscious
Nervous	Preoccupied
Sad	Uncomfortable

If you know why you feel this way, include this information as well. For example, "I'm fearful because I'm afraid of what others will think of me," or "I'm anxious because I might fail to meet my goals," or "I'm angry because I have to do this." Use as many pages as you need to identify your feelings and what the cause of those emotions is likely to be.

Ready to Start?

Over the next five weeks, you will become more familiar with why you procrastinate, set goals to complete the tasks you've been avoiding, and try all the exercises and strategies offered. I will be with you every step of the way. Then, when you have completed the program, you can hold on to the strategies that work best for your particular type of procrastination and make them a regular part of your life.

Takeaways

➤ There are different types and patterns of procrastination.

➤ Procrastination is usually caused by avoiding uncomfortable emotions or thoughts.

➤ Self-diagnostic tools help you better understand why you procrastinate.

➤ To identify your procrastination style and patterns

➤ To identify the tasks that cause you the most stress and prompt you to procrastinate

➤ To identify the feelings that make you want to avoid a task

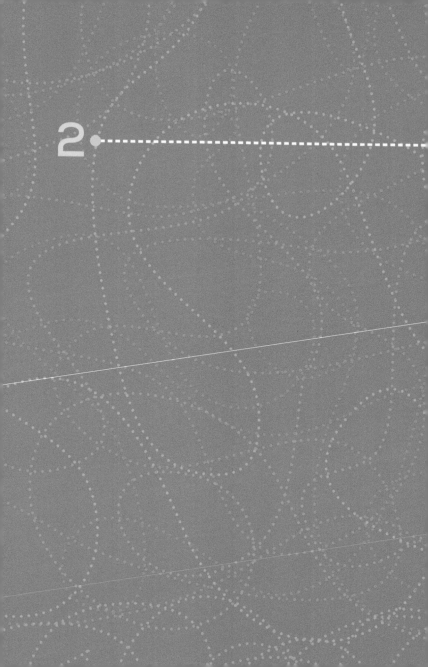

2

Week One:
Stop Avoiding and Start Achieving

What Are You Avoiding?

One of the reasons it's so hard to stop procrastinating is that it can be difficult to tell when you're doing it. Procrastinating becomes such a habit that often you don't even notice you are procrastinating. You are always busy, but somehow you never get to the really important tasks or achieve those long-term goals. If you don't know *when* you are procrastinating or *why* you are procrastinating, how can you ever hope to stop? This is where mindfulness comes into play.

In the simplest terms, mindfulness is being aware of what you're doing in the present moment. Although mindfulness has its roots in Buddhism, it has become a mainstream practice in the West and has been studied extensively for its physical and mental health benefits and been proven effective. Mindfulness is both simple to practice and a difficult skill to cultivate. Whether we're consciously aware of it or not, most of us spend a majority of our time not really focused on the present moment.

Instead, we're rehashing incidents from the past or looking ahead to the future in the form of daydreaming, planning, or anxious anticipation. With all that going on, it's no wonder something as subtle as habitual pro-crastination often doesn't rise to the level of conscious awareness.

Training yourself to become mindful of your tendency to avoid and procrastinate can help you identify when you are procrastinating. This is the first step toward putting an end to that habit for good. You can cultivate mindful-ness by grounding yourself in the present moment—what's happening here and now. This requires clearing your mind of random thoughts and worries that typically clutter it. And that's a lot harder than it sounds. However, if you follow the steps in this chapter, you will be well on your way to becoming more aware of what's happening in the moment. Let's start with some basic strategies that will get you paying more mindful attention to your goals throughout the day.

Get Aware

How do you become more mindful and self-aware of when and why you are procrastinating? The following is a series of mental steps I encourage my clients to take and that I use myself to stay aware of what it takes to progress toward important personal or career goals. These aren't steps you do once. Becoming more mindful of what's going on for you at any given moment or on any given day is a constant practice.

1. IDENTIFY YOUR DESIRED OUTCOMES

I start each day and each new project by first becoming aware of the outcomes I want to achieve. This requires some thought and decision-making. Then I create a step-by-step plan to reach each outcome. Using this approach, my work isn't *just* work—each task is a step toward important outcomes and goals I want to achieve.

By tying my activities to actual goals, I stay in touch with my motivation for getting the task done. By being more connected to the importance of what I am doing, I am more aware of when I am avoiding a given task. The same applies to the personal goals you want to achieve, such as learning a new language so that you can travel to a country you want to visit. The hard work of learning the language is tied to your strong desire to travel to that country and be able to converse with the local residents. Being aware of our desired outcomes helps us look beyond the hard work and anticipate the reward that will come when we're finished.

Throughout my day, I am continuously mindful of whether what I am working on is leading me to my desired outcome or not. I do this by constantly checking in with myself to make sure I am working toward my identified goals, which keeps me more focused *and* more motivated.

2. TAKE BACK RESPONSIBILITY FOR YOUR TIME

Are you mindful of how you spend your time? Do you think you don't have enough of it? In my coaching work, I often hear the phrase "I don't have enough time." I sympathize with the sentiment, but it's an unhelpful way to view your relationship to and influence over your own schedule. When we say, "I don't have time," we create the belief within ourselves that our time is something we have no control over.

By giving up this control to others or to general busyness, you are losing one of your most powerful options for productivity. You have more control over your time than you think, even when you work for other people. My clients often find that they double or even triple their productivity with the time-saving techniques they learn from me because they are taking personal responsibility for their time expenditures. You'll learn these techniques in later chapters, but for now, start asking yourself, *How am I choosing to spend my time in this moment?*

Running out of time is usually the result of not taking control of your own time choices. Being mindful that you have control of your time helps you make better time choices. I have a saying I use as my time management mantra and encourage my students to use as well to help them reframe their relationship with their time: **"My time, my choice."** Repeating this phrase to yourself, especially when you feel the walls of your schedule closing in on you, will remind you that you can take control of your time and you are the one making choices about how to spend it.

3. MAKE A PLAN

We usually just dive into our to-do list in the morning without giving our full awareness to planning how to get it done well and efficiently. To be more mindful of how I am going to approach my day, I apply a series of questions to the tasks on my list so I can plan how to do each one more effectively. Here are some questions I ask myself regarding each task:

- Can I dump this task?
- Can this task be automated?
- Should this task be handled by someone else?
- Is this the highest-priority task I could be working on?
- What tools, resources, or help do I need to complete this task?

Asking these questions will let you dump and automate some of your work, delegate or outsource some more, and make sure you are always working on the highest-priority task. For example, do you really need to order the supplies today? If not, dump it. Can you order your groceries online and have them delivered? You might want to give it a try.

This questioning approach also helps you gather whatever is needed ahead of time to ensure you can complete the task as soon as possible. For example, if you need some information from a colleague, request this well in advance of working on the task or else you will have an excuse to procrastinate because you need to wait for the additional information. This works for goals you want to accomplish in your personal life, too. Let's say you want to begin a diet. The tools and resources you need include the diet plan and certain types of food. Purchase them before your start date so there's no excuse to put it off any longer.

4. MEDITATE

Many people have found that a regular mediation practice helps them remain calm, boosts their awareness, and motivates them to become more productive in their daily lives. Studies have found that meditation helps improve focus and how people work together. Meditating in the morning gives you a chance to start your day feeling grounded and more at ease. Taking a few minutes to meditate when you're feeling harried can help you reset and bring your attention back to the present moment.

If you have never meditated, I recommend you attend a meditation class or watch a video to learn some of the basics. There are many types of meditation, so you will need to find a method that works best for you. For now, here is a simple 10-minute visualization meditation to start with:

1. Set a timer with a gentle tone for 10 minutes.

2. Sit down and get comfortable. There's no need to sit in a cross-legged position.

3. Breathe deeply and slowly for a couple of minutes until you notice that your breathing is even and comfortable.

4. Close your eyes and continue to breathe naturally.

5. Visualize a picture in your mind of a lovely natural setting you would enjoy being in. Build up the picture in your mind. Is there water, sand, grass? What is the sky like? What other features do you see, like rocks or trees. Keep adding detail to your mental picture.

6. Whenever your mind wanders to something else, keep bringing it back to the picture you are creating by adding more details.

7. When the timer goes off, open your eyes slowly and take a moment to adjust to an alert state before getting up.

When you first start meditating, you will likely find it difficult to keep your mind from wandering, but keep at it. You are training your brain to be more mindful of the present moment, which, among other benefits, can help when you encounter resistance to a task. If you continue this practice every day, your mind will wander less and you'll gain more awareness in general. For more help with this, see "Make a Mental Note" on page 27.

Alternatives to Meditation

If you have tried meditation for a while and still struggle with it, you can try other "mind-clearing" activities that offer similar benefits. Here are a few that I and others have found to be meditative and calming:

- Being in nature
- Cleaning
- Coloring
- Dancing
- Drawing, painting, and other forms of art
- Exercising
- Gardening
- Knitting, quilting, or crocheting
- Walking or hiking
- Whittling and wood carving

So if you just can't see yourself in a lotus position, toning and feeling your Zen, try activities that bring you to a similar place of clarity. But I do encourage you to give meditation a chance to see whether this practice might become a welcome part of your daily routine.

Make a Mental Note

As we've discussed, your mind will wander during meditation. The good news is, you make any thoughts that come up during your meditation part of your practice by "noting" them. This isn't a note-taking task. (There will be plenty of those later.) Instead, it's the practice of acknowledging your thoughts by giving them a simple one-word label without the judgments or emotional responses that draw us further from the present moment.

The label itself can be whispered or stated silently in your mind. Don't worry about the label you use; it doesn't have to be the perfect descriptive word. It can be as simple as labeling something "thinking" when you notice a thought arise. As you continue the noting practice, you will figure out for yourself what type of labels work, whether to say them aloud or whether to keep them silent. For now, choose the words that seem most appropriate, without putting too much effort into your choices.

During meditation, noting gives your mind something to do rather than granting it free rein to wander all over the place. It satisfies your mind's need to think without letting the thoughts disrupt your meditation. This keeps you present and grounded in the moment. For example, if a thought that causes you anxiety crops up, label it "anxiety" to acknowledge it and make it easier for your mind to release. You may have to repeat the label more than once until the thought naturally falls away. Don't think, *Oh, that causes me anxiety. I hate that feeling, I shouldn't feel that way,* etc. Those are all judgments. Just note "anxiety," and return to your meditation.

The idea is *not* to resolve your thoughts or make them go away, but noting does help you become more aware of the types of thoughts you are having and what types of emotions they're bringing up. In the previous chapter, you began identifying your feelings associated with procrastination. A noting practice can increase your awareness of what you're feeling. Let's say you are faced with an unpleasant task and you note "resistance" when the thought of it arises. After your noting practice, you now have a better idea of what you need to overcome to get the task done.

So far, I've only talked about noting during meditation, but this is also an active mindfulness practice you can turn to during the day. For example, you are sitting at your desk taking care of a tedious task and your thoughts turn to all the reasons you would rather not be doing it, taking your attention away from the task at hand. Instead, label it "boredom" to put your thinking mind at ease and regain your focus on getting the job done. If you are uncomfortable being bored (and who isn't?) and feeling other unpleasant emotions, the next section will help.

Get Comfortable with Discomfort

A critical part of understanding why we procrastinate is recognizing what we gain by procrastinating. Right now, you're probably thinking, *It doesn't gain me anything! All it does is cause me problems.* But if you weren't getting something out of procrastination, you wouldn't keep doing it, especially considering how much it can cost you.

One way to understand the emotional dynamics that can keep us in a procrastination loop is to think of it as a means of *emotional avoidance*. In other words, procrastination allows us, at least temporarily, to avoid some uncomfortable internal feeling like anxiety, fear, or boredom. In chapter 1, you identified some of those feelings, but are you ready to *feel* them? Sure, we can continue to avoid uncomfortable emotions for years and let them poison our lives and thoughts, but that's not the answer. We need to be willing to experience the discomfort of those feelings in order to work through them and get to the other side.

When we understand our procrastination as a means of avoidance, a whole world of solutions opens up; psychologists have been working on the problem of emotional avoidance for years. There's a branch of psychology called acceptance and commitment therapy (ACT), which teaches us to be willing to experience uncomfortable feelings and stop allowing them to derail us and prevent us from working toward things we care about. You will have a chance to do an exercise based on ACT principles in just a moment. But first, let's take a look at an example of how this might play out in the life of a *former* procrastinator, whom I'll call Renata.

Renata had to give a big presentation on a highly successful initiative she'd led, in front of her boss and several executives. She was given a week to prepare. There was no reason for her to put off preparing for a meeting that would make her look good, but she waited until she was right up against the deadline. And this wasn't the first time she'd done so. Why would Renata create avoidable problems like this for herself?

When Renata finally decided to do something about her pattern of last-minute, panic-provoking preparations, she took steps to figure out the root cause of her procrastination: *anxiety*. There was a lot riding on her performance at these meetings. Whenever she started to prep, she'd get anxious thinking about being judged by her boss and other executives. And when she felt anxious, she'd immediately stop the task that triggered her anxiety, and so the presentation just kept getting put off. What Renata eventually learned was that she didn't need to get rid of the anxiety she felt in order to prepare her presentations; she needed to learn how to be okay with the anxiety that would surface while she was preparing. With the help of ACT techniques, Renata was able to prepare for her next presentation despite the little bursts of anxiety she felt along the way. And with the extra time she put into it, it was one of her best presentations to date.

None of us can magically wish away the uncomfortable feelings associated with certain tasks—instead, we must learn to move forward even when we have uncomfortable thoughts and feelings. Since emotional avoidance plays such a large role in procrastination, to stop doing it, you have to be prepared for some discomfort as you work through the feelings *underneath* your procrastination. It won't kill you, I promise. We often learn the most and experience our greatest personal growth when we are outside of our comfort zones.

Reflection on Acceptance

Practicing acceptance is a powerful way to struggle less around uncomfortable feelings when they come up—you know, those feelings that make you want to avoid whatever it is that is causing them. Accepting something is having compassion for it, not judging it, and not trying to change it. It's a tall order, but it is possible.

Spend two to three minutes on the following steps the first time you try this exercise. You can do it for longer blocks of time if you would like once you are familiar with the process. The more you practice acceptance (rather than resisting or avoiding something), the less likely uncomfortable emotions will interfere with your ability to get important tasks done—even when they trigger anxiety.

1. Sit in a chair with your feet on the floor and get comfortable. Place your palms on your lap, and close your eyes. Breathe naturally.

2. Spend a few moments feeling the movement and rhythm of your breath, focusing on each inhale and exhale. Don't try to change anything about your breath. Just observe it and accept it as it is with kindness and compassion.

Beyond Self-Help

During this process, you might find you have strong or even overwhelming emotional reactions you feel that you can't handle. You might also suffer from chronic depression, anxiety, or other problems that are affecting your productivity and causing procrastination and other issues at work and home. In this case, seek a diagnosis, therapy, and support from a medical professional.

While the techniques in this book are supported by science, proven, and tested, some people do need medical intervention and therapy while working through their issues. Some of the clients I coach on productivity also benefit from working on other aspects of their personal and professional lives with a therapist. I always recommend seeking out additional help if you need it.

3. Notice how your back feels against the chair and how your feet feel on the floor. Notice other body sensations and the temperature of your skin. Again, don't try to change anything or judge it. Just observe and gently accept whatever physical sensations you are experiencing with kindness and compassion. You don't have to make any discomfort go away, and you don't have to focus on it either. Just observe.

4. Continue to just observe the sensations of your breath and body. As thoughts and feelings come up, consider them with kindness and compassion as well. Again, don't try to make them go away or hold on to them. Just keep observing without judgment. Be aware that you are *having* a thought or feeling, but also recognize that thought or feeling isn't who you are. If it helps, use the noting technique you learned on page 27 to label the thought or feeling to acknowledge it.

5. Allow yourself to continue to observe without judgment for a few moments before opening your eyes. When you open your eyes, make an intention to approach the project you have been procrastinating on with this same compassionate awareness.

You can do this exercise anytime you want to, but for now, have your Stop Wasting Time notebook handy. Spend a few minutes imagining that you are doing the task you have been avoiding. See yourself going through the motions even as uncomfortable feelings, like anxiety, fear, anger, and boredom, come up. Imagine acknowledging those feelings with kindness and compassion as you persist in your task and bring it to completion. Now, in your notebook, reflect on that experience:

➤ What did it look like?
➤ What feelings did it trigger?
➤ How did you act?
➤ How did you feel once the task was accomplished?

EXERCISE: Top Five Reasons to Get on with It

It helps to connect the task we are doing right now (filling out paperwork, for example) with the overall real reason we are undertaking the task (because it's part of our job and we need to make money to provide for our family). Because we value our family, filling out the paperwork that comes with the job suddenly has more meaning. Some of us might be lucky enough to find work we are passionate about and value making a contribution, but many people are just working to pay their bills. Perhaps they value the independence that working affords them even if they aren't excited about their jobs.

While you can come up with the top five reasons for any part of your life (and I encourage you to do so), let's consider now the reasons you have a job in the first place. Some reasons might be:

- ➤ To help support your family
- ➤ To experience personal growth
- ➤ To make a positive contribution
- ➤ To interact with others
- ➤ To work toward career goals
- ➤ To avoid boredom

For example, you might work part time at a low-paying job because you have young children and want to be home for them after school. In this case, you value being a parent, and this job gives you the opportunity to make some money and be available to your kids. Think along these lines to connect what you are doing professionally with what you value.

In your Stop Wasting Time notebook, title a new page "The Top 5 Reasons I Do This Work." Then give careful thought to why you have chosen to do the work, and list your top five reasons. These are all reasons to get on with the task you've been putting off.

If you are struggling with procrastination in a different area, feel free to revise your title accordingly. For example, "The Top 5 Reasons I Want to Lose Weight." Your reasons might be "to avoid weight-related disease" (because you value health), "to be around for my grandchildren" (because you value family), and so on. These are all excellent reasons to stop putting off joining an exercise class.

Fear of Failure

Fear of failure is a powerful emotional barrier that prevents us from even getting started working toward our goals. What if you try, really give something your all, and still fail? Wouldn't that be worse than not trying at all?

Fear of failure, especially in a professional context, is a rational concern. Will your manager be upset? Will you lose the respect of your colleagues? Could you even lose your job? We build this fear into long, involved worst-case-scenario lists of what could happen if we fail. Then we put off starting the task. In most cases, the terrible outcomes our minds imagine are greatly exaggerated and are unlikely to ever come to pass. Behaving as though our worst-case scenarios are real possibilities causes us more problems than it solves.

I'll give you an example from my own life: At a job where I worked, I missed completing a task that was due on a Friday and spent all weekend worrying about having missed the deadline and what the repercussions would be. The following Monday, I finished the task and gave it to my manager. He didn't say a word about its being late. I had been in emotional agony all weekend for nothing, buying in to worst-case scenarios that were, in fact, extremely unlikely to occur. Like my manager's response to my missed deadline, most things we worry about never happen. If we were to look at these imagined worst-case scenarios with an outsider's eye, it would be obvious that most of them aren't realistically going to happen.

While we all spend precious time worrying about nothing on occasion, if you regularly suffer from anxiety, seek medical help and therapy to help you deal with it. The exercises in this book can help tackle the day-to-day anxiety we all feel at times, but if you find that your anxiety is interfering with how you function on a daily basis, consider professional help.

EXERCISE: Deal with Worry

The following exercise can help you deal with your worry, especially when it comes to getting caught up in thinking about worst-case scenarios.

1. Rate the likelihood: On a scale of 1 to 10, what is the *real* likelihood that what you are worrying about is going to happen? Have you predicted similar problems in the past? How often did these other worries actually come true? How can you reduce the likelihood that what you are worried about will happen?

2. Consider all possible scenarios: We often jump to the worst-case scenario when we are worried about things, so in addition to the worst-case scenario you are envisioning, also envision a mid-range scenario and a best-case scenario. Are one of these scenarios most likely to happen?

3. Figure out ways to deal: If the worst-case scenario actually comes to pass, how would you deal with it? Having systems in place for even the worst-case scenarios can help ease your worry because you will have a plan in place to deal with it if it actually happens. You are a lot more capable than you probably think!

A failure at work can be a learning experience rather than the career-ending nightmare you might imagine. Not doing an assigned task at all runs a much higher risk of upsetting your manager and, in extreme cases, could result in you losing your job. After all, if you won't even attempt the work, why shouldn't they bring in someone who can? The same is true for failing in any area of your life. If you don't try, you'll never reap the rewards of success, and if you do fail, you have learned a valuable lesson: Try a different approach next time.

Fear of Success

Fear of failure makes sense, but why would someone fear success? Fear of success often happens when we are apprehensive about what comes after we have successfully accomplished a task or goal. We might ask ourselves questions like:

- If I succeed at this, will this raise the bar to an unstainable level?
- Will I attract more notice and higher expectations?

- Will my coworkers think I am currying favor with the higher-ups?
- Will I get promoted beyond my abilities?
- Will I be so busy that I won't have time for my family?
- What will be left for me to do if I succeed at this?

A common concern is that success will lead us into new uncharted territory. We might work with people at a higher level in the company than we did before. We might feel more exposed, under more pressure, or under more scrutiny, and we may not be prepared to deal with it. When we are insecure, success can seem nearly as scary as failure. Once again, this fear is usually blown out of proportion.

If you succeed at something, it usually isn't just luck—it is generally because you are capable or skilled at that task. When this is the case, you will most likely be able to replicate the success of similar tasks assigned to you in the future, especially as you gain experience. Always remember that it is your choice to do more and achieve more. For example, you don't have to accept a promotion if the new role doesn't fit your skills and aspirations. But also keep in mind that you can learn new skills by:

- Trying new things
- Taking courses at a local college
- Taking online courses
- Seeking out online tutorials
- Getting support from software or tool providers

➤ Getting help in forums (I love this technique. I post questions to online forums and get multiple helpful replies by the next day.)

EXERCISE: Downward Arrow Technique

For this exercise, we are using a technique from cognitive behavioral therapy (CBT). CBT is an effective form of talk therapy and behavioral therapy that helps reframe negative thinking patterns into positive thoughts that will eventually lead to positive actions.

The Downward Arrow technique helps you take control of your casual and (especially if your brain works like mine) chaotic thoughts by exploring them more fully in order to get to the root of your negative thoughts and decide if they are realistic.

Here is how this works: In your Stop Wasting Time notebook, title a new page "Negative Thought." Keep the notebook nearby. When you find yourself having a negative thought, write it down. After you've written it down, draw a downward arrow to the next line and write why that thought matters to you. Then draw another downward arrow and write why you are worried about this. Doing this helps you go deeper into the thought or emotion. Keep going downward until you get to the end, or root, of the problem.

Here is an example from my past when I found myself putting off tasks that would lead to my being able to teach workshops:

I don't want to speak in front of people.

↓

Other speakers look so much more attractive than I do.

↓

I don't like how I look.

↓

I'm fat and ugly.

↓

People will reject me because I'm not attractive enough.

↓

I am afraid of being rejected.

This example is obviously an emotional obstacle I managed to overcome, as I have spoken to thousands of people at events and workshops. And, no, I didn't suddenly become movie-star handsome with an ultra-fit body overnight. I've realized that audiences respond to me and enjoy my seminars even though I don't look like Brad Pitt.

But I found the root of the problem—I didn't like my appearance and believed I would be rejected because I felt fat and ugly. Once I had identified this problem, I started to work out techniques to improve my thinking and emotional reactions related to this belief. Most important, I didn't let my underlying, irrational fear hold me back from doing the work I love. Try this technique whenever you have negative thoughts until you find the root of each problem.

EXERCISE: Reframing Negative Thoughts

At some point you've probably had people pushing "power of positive thinking" and "think and grow rich" types of mumbo jumbo on you, suggesting that all you must do is think the right way and you'll magically become healthy and wealthy overnight. *Yeah, right.* Changes in health and finances require work, not just optimism. But there's still something to be said for positive thinking, especially when you consider its opposite: negative thinking.

Negative thinking is like a poison eating away at your self-confidence and emotional well-being. How can you succeed and be productive when there is always that inner critic whispering how incompetent or undeserving you are? When we're caught up in negative thinking, we focus on every bad thing that's happened and filter out all the good things that have happened. By applying a negativity filter, we are setting ourselves up for a bad experience.

Think of it like a "glass half full versus glass half empty" paradox. Both are technically correct, but we can choose how we view the glass. Likewise, we can choose a positive or negative perspective. It has been proven that smiling, even when you aren't happy, actually makes you happier over time. Similarly, we need to shut down the inner critic by replacing a nasty internal audio soundtrack with more powerful, positive thoughts.

Remember that thoughts are not facts. When I thought I was not worth listening to because I was fat and ugly, I worried it would matter if I wasn't the most attractive person in the world. Would people still listen to me if I had something worth speaking about? By becoming more positive about my self-image, I built a successful career as a speaker. The knowledge and passion I shared with my audience far outweighed my looks. And everyone loves my "Captain Time" hat—a steampunk-style brown hat with clock-faced goggles that's part of my ensemble.

So let's reframe some negative thoughts as positives—both may be true, but you can choose which one to focus on. In your Stop Wasting Time notebook, title a new page "From Negative to Positive." Draw a line down the center of the page. Label the first column "Negative" and the second column "Positive." Then list the negative thoughts you've noticed lately. Across from each negative, think of a positive. Here are some examples to get you started.

NEGATIVE	POSITIVE
I screwed up on a task.	I accomplished many other tasks today flawlessly. The one mistake is easily corrected. And I won't make that mistake again.
My boss criticized my work. I am a failure.	My boss provided feedback that will help me do a better job on that task next time.
I'm fat and ugly, so I will never find love.	I have many appealing physical traits. To accentuate them, I can work with an image consultant to update my wardrobe and learn how to present myself better.
I hate the feel of my office.	My office is a safe place to work. I can add artwork or change the lighting to make this space look better.

Being kind to yourself is one of the most powerful boosts to your self-image you can cultivate. To pull myself back on track from negative thoughts, I often use mantras—phrases that remind me to think in productive ways. Here is one mantra I like to use: **"Creating the life I want, with every thought, with every action."** I find this useful because it reminds me to continually ask myself, *Is this thought or action creating the life I want?* If the answer is no, I shift my energy toward the thoughts and actions that will get me where I want to go.

In your Stop Wasting Time notebook, title a new page "Action Plan: One Task." Then think about some of the tasks you have been putting off. Choose one of those tasks and write that task below the title. Using what you've learned so far, identify what emotion or potential outcome you have been avoiding by *not* doing this task and jot that down, too. Practice accepting any uncomfortable emotions that come up for you as you commit to doing this task by following the techniques in this chapter. Now, with this in mind, create an action plan to get started on this task first thing tomorrow. Here is an example of how this action plan might look if you want to ask for a raise:

Action Plan: One Task

Task: Ask for a Raise

Fear of confrontation; fear of losing my job; fear of rejection

My strategy: Create a step-by-step plan to build a case for why I deserve a raise and develop a pitch. My action steps will include:

1. Find comparable wage information.

2. Put together a list of my achievements.

3. Prepare my pitch.

4. Practice delivering my pitch.

5. Get feedback from a mentor/trusted colleague on my pitch.

6. Schedule a meeting with my manager to deliver my pitch.

With a task like this, it's unlikely you will get all of this done in one day, and that's okay. Having an action plan in place will help you take steady steps toward your desired outcome. If your task is involved like this one, set aside a half hour to an hour each day to work toward getting this done. If it is less involved, you may need to work on it only 15 minutes a day—or perhaps your task *is* something that can be accomplished in a single day. In this example, you would use your blocks of time to build a strong case for why you should be given a raise. A task like this could be completed within a week by devoting your time to each of the smaller tasks every day.

When you have your plan in place, start on the first step tomorrow. Yes, it may make you feel uncomfortable, but continue to take the next step anyway, until the task is complete.

Takeaways

➤ Becoming self-aware and mindful is the first step to ending procrastination.

➤ There will always be discomfort, and success comes when we learn how to work through the discomfort.

➤ Finding the real root reasons why you are procrastinating helps you design strategies to deal with them.

YOU LEARNED HOW:

➤ To become more mindful while accomplishing tasks

➤ To analyze a task and find the underlying reason you are avoiding it

➤ To get comfortable with being uncomfortable

➤ To replace negative thoughts with positive ones to move forward

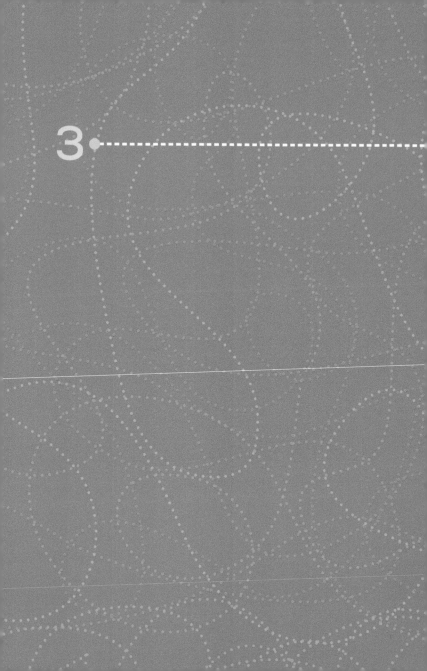

3

Week Two:
Build Your Superstructure

In engineering, a "superstructure" is a structure built on something else, such as the masts and rigging above a ship's deck that hold the sails that power the ship forward. Similarly, I am going to help you build a "success superstructure" over your existing schedule to make sure your important tasks are completed and "powered forward" like the ship.

People who are more successful and more productive than you aren't brighter or more talented. They just have better systems in place to help them sail along. Successful people don't just work hard; they have superstructures that support their success. A successful system of support is much more powerful and impactful on your day's productivity than working more hours to try to catch up. Your success superstructure helps you by:

➤ Creating a central place to keep and organize your tasks and notes

➤ Providing systems for dealing with subordinates, management, outsourced work, and coworkers; in the case of personal life, hired and volunteer help as well as family members

- Keeping you focused on the task at hand
- Reducing distractions
- Getting you past obstacles
- Providing a path to combat avoidance that leads to procrastination

Having your own success system in place makes it much easier to get into a high-productivity flow, achieve your outcomes, and stop wasting time on other things. The system helps you beat procrastination by making sure your top-priority task is always next.

At this point, many marketers would now "suggest" that you buy their amazing $2,997 "system" consisting of a software bundle and "secret blueprint" training package that you *need* to be truly successful. Well, I guess I'm missing my opportunity to cash in big because I'm going to show you how to build your own success system using an inexpensive notebook, pen, and some optional free apps and programs.

How to Build Your Superstructure

What does a task-completing superstructure look like? You already have a schedule of when you have to be at work or when your day starts in general. The superstructure is a separate "get things done" schedule that designates when each category of tasks is to be done.

With a little tweaking, you can also apply this to household tasks and personal responsibilities and goals. The superstructure will account for deadlines and due dates, as well as priorities and task importance.

Step 1: Learn to Triage

In the medical field, triage is when you quickly assess patients in a busy emergency room or disaster situation to ensure the most critical patients get help first. A patient with a broken arm can wait a bit, while a heart attack victim needs immediate help. Similarly, when you do a "task triage," you are going to look at your outstanding tasks to identify which are the most important tasks and which can be tackled later. You do this by assigning priority levels and due dates to each item.

It is important to remember during task triage that you don't "do" any tasks—rather, you are just sorting and prioritizing them to get them in order for future work. These decisions should be incredibly quick—don't agonize over each task or start thinking about how to do it. Think of it as the same system you might use for sorting laundry; you just throw each type of clothing into its own basket without thinking about it too much. Step 2 will help you set priorities and decide which "baskets" to keep your task in.

Step 2: Workflow

Every day, you get a steady flow of new tasks. If you always work on the newest ones first, the oldest ones never get done. If you work on them strictly in the order they come in, the oldest ones get done first, but new, urgent tasks wait too long. Instead, you need a system where the highest-priority tasks are identified during your triage, so they get completed first.

Let's start by figuring out what type of labeling to use for your tasks. If you already have a task management system with built-in priority levels, you can use it, but otherwise, here are two options:

OPTION 1	OPTION 2
Urgent	5
High	4
Medium	3
Low	2
Optional	1

For option 1, you label any tasks as "Urgent" that have to be done right away. "High" should be for tasks that are high priority, "Medium" for medium priority, etc. Option 2 gives you a numerical hierarchy where 5 is the highest priority and 1 is the lowest, or optional.

Usually very few tasks should be urgent. No more than 10 percent of your tasks are likely in the urgent or high (5 or 4) levels at any given time. Once you have your tasks sorted into priority sequence, you would work on all the urgent tasks until complete, then move to the high ones. If you get through all the high tasks, then you move on to medium, then low.

At work, you may need to get your manager's help with choosing your highest-priority tasks. If you don't have access to the big picture, you may assume a task is higher or lower priority than it really is and miss getting key tasks done. Ask your manager to assign a priority level to all new tasks and due dates, if appropriate. This will make it easier in the future. At home, this decision can be made alongside any other decision-makers in your household.

Due dates can also impact where a task falls in your daily workflow. Perhaps a task is only a medium priority but has a key due date of next Thursday. Assuming it will take one hour to complete, you should modify its priority level to high on next Wednesday or urgent on Thursday if it is not completed before these times.

If you are a manager or delegate tasks to others, it is best to delegate tasks to your team *first* before you work on your own top-priority tasks. This gets other people working on their project contributions, and the entire team is able to be productive without getting held up waiting for tasks or input from you.

When assigning or receiving tasks, it helps to have all the information on hand that you need to complete them. Here is an example of what you should be including when assigning tasks or what you should ask for when receiving tasks:

- ➤ Task name
- ➤ Due date
- ➤ Priority level
- ➤ Assignee (person assigned to complete task)
- ➤ Task manager (person responsible to review completed task)
- ➤ Task instructions (details of what the task involves)
- ➤ Task category (such as data entry, marketing, human resources, clients, etc.; this helps you ensure you are spending enough time on each of your roles)
- ➤ Attachments/materials (if needed to complete tasks)
- ➤ Training resources (links to training videos or documents on how to do the task; I maintain a video library of common tasks to aid my virtual assistants)

If working manually with your tasks in a notebook, you can create a column for each of these. Most common task management systems can handle these fields, or you can set up a simple table in Microsoft Excel (or any spreadsheet software) or your word-processing program for this. If you would like to use a digital task management system, here are a few free ones you can start with:

Trello: A visual drag and drop card system where each task is a card; handles priority levels, due dates, and assigning team members.

Airtable: A versatile "database meets spreadsheet" system that can be customized for nearly any use. I use it as a task management system, customer relationship management system, speaking opportunities database, editorial calendar, and for many other uses. I also create Airtable bases for my client projects so they can see the project status at a glance.

Trello works well for people who like a more visual system, and Airtable is more flexible for people who want greater customization of views. There are lots of other task management systems out there, but either of these two will be enough to get you started. If you use them for some months and find you need more features, you can look at other programs.

When looking at task management systems, it really helps to have a system that works on multiple devices. In my case, I can access my task system on my desktop computer, laptop, tablet, and smartphone. So no matter where I go or what device I have on hand, I can work on tasks, update tasks, take notes, and manage my day and my team members. Both Trello and Airtable support desktop and mobile apps.

Step 3: Single-Tasking

Multitasking is a myth. Scientific studies have proven that even acknowledged masters of multitasking get more done when they are allowed to focus on a single task at a time instead. Multitasking cripples productivity and makes you more susceptible to procrastination. That's because when we multitask, we really aren't doing more than one thing at a time—we have tiny bits of micro-focus scattered across many tasks. This scattered focus means that each task isn't getting our full attention, and that leads to shoddy work. And continuously micro-focusing on the smaller, easier tasks tempts us to continue avoiding the larger, more difficult tasks. What's the alternative? Single-tasking.

Once you have prioritized your tasks, focus on *only* the top-priority task with a singular focus and work on it until it's done. Then move to the second-most-important task until it's done, and so on. One great way to single-task is to set a countdown timer for 30 minutes and then just work on one task until it's done or until the timer is finished. If you finish the first task in 5 minutes, move to the second task, and keep going until the full 30 minutes are up. Then, after the 30 minutes, take a 5-minute stretch break, reset the timer for another 30 minutes, and move to the next-most-important task. Continue this way until you've completed your tasks. This technique is known as the Pomodoro Technique. It was named after a tomato-shaped kitchen timer (*pomodoro* is "tomato" in Italian) used by the original developer of the technique in the late 1980s—a university student named Francesco Cirillo.

You can use an online timer from a website or on your smartphone, or a simple kitchen timer (tomato shape optional) from a dollar store. I use the standard clock app that comes with my phone. There are also many other smartphone timer apps to try.

Learning how to focus on a single task at a time is probably *the* biggest positive impact you can make on your productivity, which goes a long way toward curbing your tendency to waste time doing everything or anything else. When you're being productive, you will be motivated to keep up the good work.

Step 4: Create Your Day's Superstructure

In your Stop Wasting Time notebook, title a new page "Tomorrow's Superstructure." Use your calendar for tomorrow as a starting base. Begin with time-scheduled items you are committed to, such as meetings and when you have your lunch break. With the remaining time, set aside time blocks to take care of the tasks you have identified as urgent or high.

It is usually more efficient to work in batches. For example, if you need to write an article, it makes sense to work for 30 minutes to an hour on writing rather than writing for 5 minutes, checking or sending an e-mail, making a phone call, etc. Here are some example categories of time blocks with some possible examples of each:

- Planning
  - Planning your outcomes/day/week/tasks and priorities
- Product development
  - Writing
  - Product planning
  - Product creation

- Marketing
  - Creating marketing plan
  - Assigning marketing tasks
  - Monitoring results
- Human resources
  - Recruitment
  - Training
  - Performance management and coaching
- Client service
  - E-mail replies
  - Phone calls and call returns

So, based on these time blocks, a day's superstructure might look like this:

TOMORROW	TIME BLOCKS
9:00 a.m.	Client service
10:00 a.m.	Marketing
11:00 a.m.	Human resources
Noon	Lunch
1:00 p.m.	Product development
2:00 p.m.	Meeting
3:00 p.m.	Human resources
4:00 p.m.	Planning

It is critical to remember that you will be working on the highest-priority task in each category during that designated time block. So in this example, you will be doing the most important client replies during the "Client service" block and the top-priority marketing tasks during the "Marketing" block of time. I have used one-hour time blocks here, but you can work with half-hour blocks, two-hour blocks, divide your days into morning and afternoon focuses, or set laser-focus days where you spend the entire day on something like writing or marketing.

Wondering how to apply this to your personal life and weekends? You can also use a superstructure to get more things done at home and still schedule time for fun. On the next page is a similar table showing how this might look.

SATURDAY	TIME BLOCKS
9:00 a.m.	Clean out garage
10:00 a.m.	Clean out garage
11:00 a.m.	Get ingredients at grocery store for supper with friends
Noon	Lunch
1:00 p.m.	Walk/fitness
2:00 p.m.	Straighten living room
3:00 p.m.	Start cooking
4:00 p.m.	Friends arrive
5:00 p.m.	Serve supper
6:00 p.m.	Relax with friends

By setting aside time for your fun, such as time with friends, date nights, and "adventure" days, you can make sure you enjoy your life while getting more done.

Where Does E-mail Fit In?

Ever see the TV show *Hoarders*, where people have so much stuff in their homes that they can hardly move around and their health is affected? Some of us have the digital clutter equivalent of these hoarders' physical accumulations—especially in our e-mail inbox. And just like those hoarders, it affects our mental health and stress levels.

We spend a *lot* of time in our e-mail inbox, and it can feel overwhelming to see a huge list of unopened and unanswered e-mails waiting for us. Cluttered and disorganized e-mail inboxes aren't your fault. The way the e-mail system works is that every e-mail sent to you arrives in the same place. So an e-mail from a prospect about an upcoming huge deal is treated the same way in the system as a joke forwarded by a friend, a notice about an upcoming event you don't have to worry about for months, or even e-mails asking you to buy something (spam).

All of my e-mail is dealt with every day, and my e-mail inbox is clean. And I don't work overtime to do it. Sounds impossible, doesn't it? It's not. I'm going to show you a technique that takes no more than 20 minutes a day that will solve your e-mail clutter problems. This technique, known as the Zero E-mail Inbox technique, will work no matter what e-mail system you are using. Take a look:

Zero E-mail Inbox Steps

The Zero E-mail Inbox technique gives you a system for quickly finding your high-priority e-mails, organizing your e-mails so you can easily retrieve them, and ending the day with an empty inbox. Here are the steps.

1. **E-mail triage:** Sort e-mails into categories and priority levels (discussed next).

2. **Delete and dump:** Delete any noncritical e-mails and empty your trash folder.

3. **Delegate:** Forward e-mails that can be handled by others to an appropriate point person and ask for the matter to be handled. Then either delete or archive the e-mail for later retrieval, as necessary.

4. **Respond:** Answer e-mails according to priority level as efficiently as possible and archive them for later retrieval, if necessary.

E-MAIL TRIAGE (SORTING)

E-mail crosses multiple categories and priority levels. In your work e-mail, you might have e-mails from clients, managers, the human resource department, the sales department, colleagues, etc. In your personal e-mail, you might have e-mails from friends, charities, community groups, credit cards, etc. (Hopefully you have separate e-mail accounts for each.) Just like normal tasks, these e-mails should be "triaged" the same way.

This can be done by using folders, labels, tags, or categories depending on the type of e-mail program you use. Instead of working on your e-mails from your e-mail inbox, you triage them into the appropriate folders/labels/categories. Create sorting folders in your e-mail for:

Now: e-mails to be worked on first

Next: next-level e-mails

Pending: e-mails you are waiting for more information to deal with

Reading: e-mails for reading only, such as newsletters

Archive: e-mails that are finished

Do you have a person whose e-mails are higher priority than others? A person like your largest client or your manager? You can automatically forward all e-mails from that person into the "Now" folder to make sure they get your priority attention by using the filter function on your e-mail program.

If an e-mail has a future due date on it, I recommend adding it to your task list with a due date. Alternatively, you could add the future e-mail to your "pending" folder and make sure you have a task set to check your "pending" folder once or twice a week. There are also tools like Boomerang for Gmail that let you archive your messages and have them come back into your inbox on a date you choose.

All of these techniques will work, but you need to ensure you have a set system you are using and stick to it. Personally, I just add the e-mail to my task management list along with a link to the original e-mail. Explore the e-mail program you use to see what tools you have available, and start putting them to good use.

When you have your folders in place, move your e-mails to their respective new homes. Don't agonize over each one; the decisions need to be made quickly, within a few seconds each. You can also recover e-mails later if you make a mistake. Try not to open the whole e-mail in most cases; instead just drag it to "Now," "Next," or "Pending" based on who it is from and the subject line. Handle each e-mail *only once* right now. Either delete, schedule, or put it in the appropriate folder to deal with in order of priority.

Your Inbox Is *Not* a Storage Place

Delete e-mails you no longer need, and empty your e-mail trash. Make sure all the important e-mails in your "Now," "Next," and "Pending" folders are dealt with by either responding or delegating, and then archive them. Don't keep one-thousand-plus e-mails in your inbox. Using the Zero E-mail Inbox technique, your e-mail inbox will come to zero every day.

You can turn e-mails into tasks by adding them to your task list in priority sequence. This way, you don't have a separate task list and e-mail task list. Gmail, for example, has a button that can be added to your browser to easily add tasks to the project management app Trello.

Personal versus Work E-mail

To help keep your work and personal life separate so that neither takes your focus away from the other, I highly recommend keeping separate accounts for your work and personal e-mail. A separate personal e-mail account prevents you from seeing and obsessing about work during your personal time in your evenings and on weekends. It also helps keep your personal life private from your work colleagues and manager.

By checking only your personal e-mail during personal time, you can reply to friends and family more thoughtfully. If your personal e-mail inbox is overflowing, you can apply the Zero E-mail Inbox technique to get it under control.

Apps and Other Automated E-mail Managers

There are lots of apps and automated systems to help you manage your e-mail. Let's take a look at some of the tools I use every day, which you may find work for you, too.

TEXT EXPANDER SOFTWARE

Personally, I use the text expander software called PhraseExpress to automate my e-mail replies and document creation. There are other versions, including WordExpander and Breevy, and they all do basically the same thing: They let you create common replies and insert them into any e-mail, form, or document with just a few keystrokes. The specific functions you get will vary depending which software you choose, but with a quick Internet search, you can find product descriptions and customer reviews to help you decide which expander will best suit your needs.

E-MAIL LIST MANAGEMENT

In addition to my one-on-one e-mails, I also work with one-to-many communications via e-mail. This lets me:

- Build lists of people by interest category
- Allow people to *automatically* access content, sign up for events, subscribe, and unsubscribe
- Broadcast to thousands of people who have signed up and are eagerly wanting to receive my content
- Send out a series of automated e-mails to inform people about an event
- Send out a product launch sequence of e-mails to bring people to my sales funnel

The tool I use to manage my e-mail list automation is MailerLite. It is inexpensive and easy to use. An e-mail list management and broadcast tool is critical for keeping in touch with my subscribers, and most of my income comes from communications with my list.

FILTERING

I use filters in Gmail to automatically sort e-mails based on who they are from. (This also works in Outlook and most other e-mail programs.) E-mails can be sent directly to my "Reading" folder without ever hitting my inbox. This filtering also lets me set priority levels and clean up spam. You can also use filtering to make sure important e-mails go into your "Now" folder automatically to save time sorting.

Your Daily To-Dos

A to-do list is at the heart of ending procrastination and getting more done. A to-do list does this by:

- Acting as a central capture point for all your tasks
- Helping you assign priority levels and due dates
- Keeping you focused on the next task at hand
- Ensuring you don't forget important tasks so nothing falls through the cracks
- Tracking what you have done for the day, which gives you a measure of your daily productivity
- Giving you a feeling of accomplishment as you cross off each task

To-Do List Capture

Do you constantly find yourself saying, "I have to remember to do (fill in the blank)"? Often an hour or two later, you are racking your brain trying to remember what that important task was. Our memory is an unreliable place to keep a to-do list. Committing to using a written or digital to-do list gives you a system to quickly and easily capture these tasks as they occur to you.

You can also use simple, physical mnemonic triggers to increase your awareness of what to work on and to pull yourself back on track. For example, one of my clients had a successful podcast that created a lot of engagement with the community she was reaching. But many community members would call her up just to chat with no real purpose in mind other than socializing. Their conversations would go on and on, tying up her time while not creating any additional revenue for her. So we created a very simple mnemonic for her—yellow sticky notes on her computer screen and phone that read *Who is paying for this time?* The yellow sticky notes had a huge impact by reminding her to politely cut unproductive calls short so she could get back to her paying work.

Why Make a Daily To-Do List?

You need to commit to using your to-do list as part of your productivity system and use it every day. If you stop using your system, your system can't help you avoid procrastination and wasting time. Even if you have only two things to do today, you should still write them down (in priority sequence) and add them to your to-do list and mark them off. This way you can start building the habit, and when you have more items on your list, you already have a system in place.

Keep It Running

Think of your daily to-do list as a living document. You will be continually capturing new tasks, highlighting important tasks, and crossing off tasks as they are completed. Just as you would pay attention to a living creature in your care, you need to pay attention to your to-do list.

Review your to-do list at the end of each day. Add today's leftover tasks to the next day's to-do list along with tomorrow's tasks. Determine your priorities at the end of today, and you can start tomorrow fresh and secure in the knowledge of what your priorities are and what you need to work on first thing in the morning. It takes the guesswork out of the day ahead.

Check Yourself—To-Do List Commitment

When people first start a to-do list or any new system, they pay attention to it for the first while but then usually fall back into old habits—like forgetting to check the to-do list, forgetting to add new tasks to it, and relying on their memory for what to do next. Then they lose the many benefits of the to-do list, such as clear priorities, focus, and ensuring nothing falls through the cracks.

Like a new diet or fitness regimen, you benefit from your new to-do list system *only* when you stick to it every day. So do regular rechecks. Check your list first thing in the morning to see which priority task to work on. When you get back from lunch, check again to make sure you are still working in priority sequence. After each task completion, interruption, phone call, bathroom break, etc., check the list to see what's next.

Make sure you don't start *any* task without first consulting your list to see what the next priority task is. Don't start any *new* task until you add it to your to-do list and give it a priority level. Your to-do list is your productivity "holy book." Commit to it! Have faith that it will help.

Here are a couple of simple to-do list formats to try. These are job-related examples, but they also work for any type of to-do list. There are also many apps that have preset task templates, but these simple to-do lists can be easily set up in a notebook or on an electronic spreadsheet.

Example 1: Numbered Priority List

In this example, you simply list your tasks in priority sequence:

1. Toilet paper for bathroom (we all know why this is top priority)

2. Create agenda for tomorrow's marketing meeting

3. Return phone calls

4. E-mail replies

5. Review applications for new hire

6. Brainstorm new product idea with team

7. Consider request to appear on *Dancing with the Stars*

This is a very simple but effective system. Remember to not just add tasks at the top because they are easy or because you like them—the number one item on the list should be the top priority, regardless of the complexity.

You can rewrite and revisit the priorities once per day. Some people leave room at the top or between items on their list in case a new, higher-priority task comes up. Alternatively, you can write the new task at the bottom and highlight it. But then you would need to remember to also check the bottom of your list!

Example 2: Time Block To-Do List

Remember earlier when we talked about time blocking to set aside time for each of your roles? Here is what a to-do list sorted by time blocks might look like:

- Administrative
  - Toilet paper for bathroom
- Human Resources
  - Review applications for new hire
- Client Services
  - Return phone calls
  - E-mail replies
- Marketing
  - Create agenda for tomorrow's marketing meeting
  - Consider request to appear on *Dancing with the Stars*
- Product Development
  - Brainstorm new product idea with team

Same idea, but you just sort the tasks into their categories and work on them in priority sequence during the category time blocks. You don't actually start at the top of the list for this one. Instead, you look at your time block on your calendar. If it is your marketing block, you would start with the first task under "Marketing," which is to create the agenda for tomorrow's marketing meeting. This is the system I use—gathering tasks under time-block categories and then working on them in priority sequence.

Digital Task Lists versus Written To-Do Lists

I mentioned earlier that some people use software or apps to organize their to-do lists while others use written notepads, journals, or agendas. To help you figure out what might be the best method for you, here are some pros and cons of each:

PHYSICAL (WRITTEN) PLANNER	
PROS	**CONS**
Writing helps you remember and learn	Possibility of loss
	Difficult to share calendar
Different designs for different needs	Difficult to assign tasks to others
No power needed	
Gives you a tech break	

SOFTWARE (DIGITAL) PLANNER	
PROS	**CONS**
Easy to share	Needs power/charging
Can access on multiple devices	May not synchronize in areas without data coverage
Phone version always with you	Tied to technology
No concerns about loss	
Can delegate within system	
Some are customizable to meet your needs	

My first time management tool was a Day-Timer—a physical, agenda-style planner. As I mentioned in the introduction, it was a wonderful gift from my manager at the time. My Day-Timer worked very well for me for many years. Later, as I started managing remote teams, I switched to software planners, but I miss my physical Day-Timer occasionally.

To organize yourself, either a written or digital method of keeping your to-do lists will work, but if you need to manage a larger team or work with remote team members, I recommend a software planner like the aforementioned Trello or Airtable (see pages 54 and 55).

Week Two: Action Plan

In your Stop Wasting Time notebook, title a new page "Tomorrow's Superstructure." Refer back to the first time you did this exercise on page 57. This is an activity you will do again and again—on a daily basis, in fact, starting now.

Create either a time block to-do list or a numbered priority list for tomorrow. You can try the opposite of what you did previously to see which works best for you. The idea is to make sure you can easily see the highest-priority item to work on first, mark it complete, and then move on to the second-most-important task, and so on. Using what you've learned in this chapter, create a schedule for tomorrow that allots time to each of the tasks you need to accomplish. Don't forget to schedule time for the Zero E-mail Inbox technique.

If you would like to, you can now look at putting this information into a software program or app, but don't let a search for the perfect software solution give you an excuse to procrastinate on taking action. If you don't already have a good idea of which tool you will use, use your physical notebook for now. If you would like to research the choices available, add that to tomorrow's to-do list, and schedule it for after all your higher-priority tasks.

Be sure to look at your schedule first thing tomorrow morning. If need be, place a sticky note on your computer monitor or even on your bathroom mirror to remind yourself to look at your to-do list before you get going.

From now on, set aside a block of time at the end of each day to create your superstructure for tomorrow.

Takeaways

➤ Success comes from having a good productivity system.

➤ A daily to-do list is the key system to stop wasting time and end procrastination.

➤ Working in priority sequence maximizes your productivity and helps you avoid procrastination.

➤ Your e-mail inbox is for sorting, not for working on and filing e-mails.

➤ Multitasking doesn't work—single-focusing on each task is more efficient.

YOU LEARNED HOW:

➤ To create a daily to-do list

➤ To prioritize your tasks

➤ To better focus and work on a single task at a time

➤ To commit fully to your to-do list as your primary productivity system

➤ To bring your e-mail inbox to zero every day

➤ To treat your to-do list as a living document, continually updating and refreshing it for the next day

4

Week Three:

Deal with Time Bandits

What Steals Your Time?

Time is very valuable—more valuable than money. Think about it. If you run out of money, you can always find ways to save, earn, or borrow more to get you through. But if you run out of time—that's it, you're out of luck. You can't earn more time or borrow time from somebody else! Even the wealthiest person cannot buy another year of time with all their money when they are on their deathbed. In that sense, time is priceless.

But time is similar to money in that it's a commodity you need to conserve, and it's something that can be taken from you if you're not careful. Just like your money can be stolen by thieves, your time can be stolen, too, by what I call "time bandits." You need to beware of the time bandits in your environment—those people and activities that eat up your valuable time and keep you from getting to the "real" tasks you want to accomplish! Let's start by looking at some common time bandits, and then

I'll help you figure out how to minimize them or banish them completely.

Other People

I like to think of my time in a day as 24 golden coins that I have to spend. I am very careful in how I spend my time coins, and I don't let other people, random tasks, or my electronic devices steal my coins and spend my time for me in ways I wouldn't choose to spend it myself. Let's start by looking at some of the ways that other people can spend your time and interfere with your productivity:

- Requests for help
- Socializing and gossip
- Unfocused conversations with no specified goals
- Meetings
- Unplanned phone calls
- Personal phone calls during work time
- Work calls during personal time

We interact with people continuously in our work and personal lives, so learning how to deal with people more efficiently has a huge impact on our productivity. Think of how many times each day you speak to a colleague, subordinate, or manager. Think of how many meetings you have to attend and how much of your time this ties up each week. Many offices are now embracing an "open concept" where people work in a communal environment out in the open instead of in separate offices or cubicles.

While the idea behind open offices is to improve collaboration, studies have shown that the open office concept actually reduces productivity.

Interactions with other people take up a lot of your day, so learning how to make these interactions more productive is key to your success in improving your productivity and keeping you focused on the tasks you need to accomplish.

Media and Devices

It used to be that we only had to worry about phone calls and people interrupting us. Over the past couple of decades, that list of interruptions has greatly expanded. In addition to phone calls and in-person interruptions, we now have to contend with interruptions from:

- Apps and programs
- E-mail
- Online calendars
- Smartphones
- Social media
- Task management systems
- Team collaboration tools
- Text messages
- Video calls

Worse yet, our smartphones are with us virtually all the time, so we get calls, e-mails, social media updates, text messages, and other notifications throughout the day, evening, and even at night. In addition to our friends and family members who want our immediate attention, customers and managers sometimes think we should answer their phone calls, e-mails, or tweets 24/7. So we don't even get a full evening or day off anymore. The problem of being connected after work has gotten so bad that some countries such as France and Germany have legislation in place to ban employers from contacting employees outside of work hours. Not a bad idea.

Cannibal Tasks

"Cannibal tasks" are tasks that eat up the time you have set aside for other tasks. Usually this happens with open-ended projects without firm deadlines or projects with vague goals that keep expanding and eating more of your time. Here are some examples of cannibal tasks:

- Research a new training program (no set due date)
- Find out how we can improve client relationships
- Improve our hiring process
- Clean your home (ongoing, never finished)
- Improve your social life

Some of these tasks could be very important, but with no firm end dates or firm estimates of how much time you should be spending, these cannibal tasks become black holes sucking up your time coins into their endless depths. Don't let it happen.

Stealing Your Time Back

To help you steal your time back, I've put together some techniques to deal with each of these common time bandits. These are focused on the workplace, but with some modification they can apply to your home life, too, when you are trying to complete household tasks or achieve personal goals. For example, you wouldn't ask your children to put their requests in an e-mail, but you can let them know that you are busy with something, so if they have any nonemergency requests, they should save them up for later.

Other People

INTERRUPTIONS FROM PEOPLE

While interruptions in a busy office environment may seem to just be a fact of life, there are techniques to greatly reduce interruptions from people. Even if you can reduce people interruptions by only 20 percent, this will have a huge impact on your focus and productivity. Here are some ways to deal with these interruptions at work:

Respect staff reporting structure: Ensure that people approach their direct supervisor for help and guidance first instead of coming to you unless there is a reason for you to be the designated person to help.

Non-interruptive (asynchronous) communication:
Encourage non-interruptive communication via e-mail or comments within the task management program you are using instead of walking to someone's desk and physically interrupting them. For example, if someone walks into your office and interrupts you to tell you they ordered the new software you asked for, this totally destroys your focus, and it can take 20 minutes or longer to get back to the same level of focus. This information really didn't require discussion, and a simple "ordered today" note on the task or an e-mail would have been sufficient. You would still get the information you need about the status of the software order, but you would have received it when you checked on the task instead of being interrupted during time you had set aside for a different task that needed deep focus.

Manager interruptions: Is your manager constantly interrupting you with questions and status updates? Work out a system where you report updates daily via your task management system and/or with quick 20-minute update meetings. My team adds comments to each task in our task management system so I can see where they are at by just looking at a task. If I want an update, I just add a comment to the task requesting an update. This way, no one is interrupted with task questions or updates.

Schedule help time: If someone needs your help, tell them you are tied up now but will help them later in the afternoon. Suggest they schedule time with you in future when you are available to assist, or set aside a certain block of time in your day/week when people know it is okay to interrupt you for help.

Personal calls during work: I recommend that people set their personal phone calls to voice mail during work hours and check their voice mail on their coffee breaks and during lunch. The same with personal text messages. Tell immediate family members they will be unable to reach you in person during work hours unless it is an emergency. Let them know to call your work line in case of an emergency and just leave texts or voice mails on your personal phone for nonemergency communications.

Interruptions at Home

Do you get interrupted a lot at home when you are trying to focus on something you would like to accomplish? Talk to your family and let them know you are setting aside a couple of focus hours during which you will work on your project or hobby and ask them to respect that time. Or go to a library or coffee shop, if possible, to eliminate any interruptions. If family or friends often show up unannounced, let them know that it is best to organize visits ahead of time to get together. If they persist in showing up unannounced, grab your coat and say you were just on your way out to an important appointment so you don't have time right now. Hopefully they will get the message.

SOCIALIZING AT WORK

While some socializing is useful for building teams, try to move it to nonpeak work/focus times. Socialize instead during coffee breaks, lunch, work social events, or other break times. If a chatty coworker approaches you to socialize while you're working, you can use the excuse that you are facing a project deadline and arrange to meet them for lunch to talk.

UNFOCUSED CONVERSATIONS

People tend to ramble on in conversations, so you need to bring them to the point quickly. Being succinct helps you get them what they need so you can get back to your own work. This technique can be applied to customers, suppliers, coworkers, and management. Instead of open-ended questions like "How are you today?" or "How was your weekend?" use questions like "How can I help you?" or "What do you need from me for the project?" or "What is our next step?"

If someone wants to provide you with ideas for something, ask them to send you their best three ideas on the topic in writing so you can explore them further. This will make them clarify their ideas, narrow down the best ones, and send you a succinct list instead of rambling on about their ideas in an open-ended conversation.

MEETINGS

Meetings are one of the greatest time wasters in an office environment. Here are some tips for organizers to make these meetings more productive:

Set a purpose for each meeting. Don't meet just to have a meeting. There should be set goals in place specifying the problems you want to solve during the meeting, or there shouldn't be a meeting.

Always have a written agenda distributed before the meeting. Set an estimated amount of time for each agenda item so people know how much time to spend on each and how important each item is.

Set ground rules. Ground rules set out how the meeting will work and how people should act with other. Some good ground rules include respecting each other, not interrupting each other, making points quickly, no smartphones, sticking to the agenda, and being on time.

Have a capture system in place for meeting notes. This might include an audio or video recording of the meeting, meeting notes, mind maps, and smartphone pictures of whiteboards. One person at the meeting should be responsible for the capture and the creation of meeting notes.

Start on time. If some people haven't arrived yet, start anyway. This will encourage the late arrivals to be on time in the future. If people are habitually late to meetings, discuss this unacceptable behavior with their supervisor and explain how their being late is disrespectful of their colleagues' time.

Distribute any reports ahead of time in writing. This stops people from having to read the reports during the meeting. Only deal with reports by asking if there are any questions pertaining to them.

Stay focused and keep people on track. Don't let meeting attendees discuss items that aren't on the agenda or jump ahead on the agenda. If they do stray, point out what the current topic is and come back to it. Keep to the time allotted to each item on the agenda so you don't run behind.

Ensure conciseness. Teach people to make their points clearly and quickly and then pause for others to give feedback. Don't let people ramble on and on. You need a strong meeting facilitator for this.

Action plan. Create an action plan during the meeting so people know what their task takeaways are to achieve the meeting's purpose. Ensure tasks from the meeting/action plan are added to the task management system of everyone involved for follow-up.

Never ask, "Is there anything else?" If you ask this question, you have just ruined all the hard work of creating an agenda and sticking to it. If something is important enough to be discussed, it is important enough for someone to submit as an agenda item. If anyone brings up anything new, tell them you will consider adding it to the next meeting's agenda.

End on time. Set a timer at the beginning of the meeting to make sure you stay on schedule and respect everyone's time.

But what if you don't organize the meeting? What if you are just an attendee? Well, you can start by getting them a copy of this book and highlighting this section for them. You can do this anonymously if you are concerned about blowback. If you have a good relationship with the meeting organizer, suggest some of these areas for them. You can also encourage better meetings and improve your experience in them by:

- Asking for an agenda ahead of time
- Being well prepared to discuss the topics
- Making your answers clear and concise and following good ground rules even if others aren't
- Making sure your reports are all in writing and distributed ahead of time
- Gently pointing out when the meeting has gone off topic
- Making your own task list for action items directed to you during the meeting
- Being attentive and asking intelligent questions
- Using the meeting as an opportunity to show your skills and value and to build better work relationships

Media and Devices

Does a star hockey player answer their smartphone during the Stanley Cup Finals when they are on the ice and have a breakaway on their opponent's goal? Do you see a cellist in a symphony orchestra sending or reading texts while they are playing onstage? Of course not. World-class performance requires world-class focus!

Imagine you are planning at a very high level, and your brain is incredibly focused and working amazingly to solve your worst problems. Do you really want to interrupt it for a Facebook notification, text, or e-mail? How likely is it that the communication will be important enough to risk disrupting your workflow?

The truth is, you simply cannot work at a high level and maintain full focus with continual interruptions from devices and media—none of us can. We want our surgeons, nuclear power plant technicians, heavy equipment operators, hockey players, cellists, and others to work with full focus. So should you. One of the single-most-important things you can do to take back your focus and time is managing your devices more strategically. Here are some ways to tame media and device interruptions:

E-mail: Turn e-mail notifications off and make a habit of checking your e-mails a couple of times a day to see what is new. Microsoft Outlook can be especially bad for this as the program has desktop notifications that come through even when the program is closed if you don't turn them off. *Close* your e-mail tab or program while you are working on other things so you aren't tempted to peek for just a second to see what the new e-mail is.

Telephones: I understand that part of your job may be answering the phone. But, unless you are in a call center, there might be times in the day when you need to fully focus without constant telephone interruptions. In those cases, send your calls to voice mail for an hour or so and check your voice messages once your peak focus time is over.

Browser tabs: My coaching clients share their computer screens with me so I can see what they are working on and we can discuss strategies. One of the common things I see with many of my clients when they share their screen is that they might have 10 or more browser tabs open. While modern computers have enough memory to keep multiple tabs open, this is very distracting. Keep *only* the tabs open you need for the task on hand and close the rest. This will help you focus.

Social media: Twitter, Facebook, YouTube, Instagram, and other social media platforms all let you know when friends post status updates or when people comment on what you've shared on social media. These continual notifications are a constant interruption and cripple your focus. If these are personal social media activities, only open your social media and be active on them during your downtime. If social media is part of your work, such as if part of your job is to manage a social media campaign, have a set time of the day that you check and reply to all comments and posts.

Smartphones: Smartphones aren't just phones anymore; they are portable computers. A high-end, brand-name smartphone can be more expensive than many laptops. So, in addition to phone calls and texts, they also give you e-mail and social media notifications. And every app installed on your smartphone seems to think you need a notification every time something happens, so all notifications are on by default. Learn to turn off all the notifications on your smartphone except those that are really needed. I have my phone remind me of appointments but *not* new e-mails or Facebook messages or anything else. Check personal texts and calls during breaks and lunch hours instead of letting them interrupt the task you are focusing on.

For many of us, checking our smartphones has become like an addiction. If we haven't checked it in the last 10 minutes, we are concerned we might be missing something important. Also, many of our friends and even clients might have an expectation that they will hear back from us in minutes. For business, I have a standard where I reply to all e-mails, phone calls, and other communications within one business day, and I let my clients know this commitment so they can anticipate when to expect a reply. My family and friends all know I don't reply to text messages or calls during business time, so they expect to hear back from me at lunch or in the evening.

It is important to remember that your technology serves you—you don't serve your technology. Take control of all your media and devices, and let your technology interrupt you only when you need the interruption, such as in the case of remembering an appointment or to remind yourself to move on to a new project.

Cannibal Tasks

I mentioned earlier that cannibal tasks are serious time suckers. It is the open-endedness of cannibal tasks that make them dangerous. Here are some ways to stop cannibal tasks from eating other tasks' time by nailing the cannibal tasks down and stopping them from being so nebulous.

Clarify goals. Clarify the goals of the project so that you can put together a plan of tasks to complete it.

Set time limits. Make sure management is clear on how much time they want you to spend on the project. Is this a 5-hour, 25-hour, or 100-hour project? I have had cases where I wanted a virtual assistant to spend a couple of hours researching something for me, and she went ahead and spent her entire 10-hour weekly budget of time on this single task because I wasn't clear in my instructions on how much time I wanted her to spend on it. Once you know the length of the time investment management wants, you can plan accordingly.

Block time. Have a set block of time each week to work on larger, long-range projects. Spend the time block fully on this project, but don't get carried away and let it cannibalize additional time.

Break the task into modules. Break larger projects into smaller modules and make a list of tasks to complete each module.

Create your own schedule. If the project has no milestones or end date, create your own. This will help you complete the project and bring it to a close.

Your Brain Is the Biggest Time Bandit

The brain is an amazing tool. The human brain can compose symphonies, build space probes to explore the solar system, launch exciting new businesses, or at the other end of the productivity spectrum, binge-watch funny cat videos on YouTube for hours at a time.

How do we get our brains to focus on the exciting things we want to accomplish instead of squandering our precious time coins consuming brainless media or filling our days with pointless busywork? Let's figure out why our brains steal time from us so we can start taking it back.

Distraction and Inability to Focus

Our world is full of "shiny" things that are constantly competing for our attention. This can include:

Media: books, movies, TV, e-books, online videos, games

People: in-person interactions, online discussion forums, social media, opinion videos

World events: news, politics, crises, causes

With the Internet, all of this is just a click away. A simple task-related search brings up a list of potentially relevant websites, articles, and videos. But the search and related websites also show you advertising—advertising that is personalized for you based on earlier searches. So even though you were searching for something specific to your task right now, you may still get distracting information related to passions and hobbies during what should be your productivity time.

If I decide to write an article about distractions and search for the word *distractions* in Google, one of the results that comes up is a video for a song by Paul McCartney called "Distractions." As a Beatles fan, I was intrigued, so of course, I clicked the video to check out a song by Paul McCartney I had never heard before. Oops, now I am not really working on the article. And once I am in YouTube, of course it serves me up a lot of other related videos, as well as videos based on my other searches.

So how do you train your brain to focus when all of these "shiny" things are there to distract you? Here are two primary methods that can keep you focused:

Be aware of your limited willpower/discipline. Discipline sounds great in theory. It seems that if we were only more disciplined, all our procrastination problems would be solved. The problem is that we only have so much willpower and discipline we can apply to our tasks each day—it's a limited resource. After your reservoir of willpower is exhausted, your brain wants to take a break and play. By knowing that your willpower is a limited resource, you can work with this by keeping your peak focus time for the most difficult and important tasks you have. For me, my peak focus is first thing in the morning. So I schedule my most difficult tasks for the morning and keep the low-energy tasks I enjoy in the afternoon. If I work on my favorite easy tasks first, then I struggle to apply enough discipline in my low-energy afternoons to get through the more difficult tasks.

Set time blocks. I find time blocks really help keep me focused. If I have a block of time set aside for writing a book like this one, I *only* work on writing the book during that block of time. If you create focused blocks of time that are a half hour or an hour in length for a set project, task, or purpose, it is much easier to stay focused during that time.

I still consume fun media, but I have set blocks of time when I watch my favorite TV show or browse a few You-Tube videos. And, yes, even I watch the occasional funny cat video. They're so cute . . .

EXERCISE: Your Distraction Diary

A great way to reduce distractions is to keep a Distraction Diary. In your Stop Wasting Time notebook, title a new page "Distraction Diary" and include today's date. This can be the entry format you use anytime you decide this exercise will help get you focused and back on task.

With your Distraction Diary close at hand, keep a log of *every* time you stop working on the task you set for yourself. This includes *every* interruption, every time you looked up something else instead of what you were working on, every notification that distracted you, etc. This log will show you what your worst distractions are so you can start minimizing them by using the techniques and strategies you are learning. Just the act of keeping the Distraction Diary helps keep you from straying off task, because who wants a long list of distractions?

When I coach my clients, I have them keep a Distraction Diary as a diagnostic tool. In the same way a doctor takes vital signs to determine a patient's overall health and issues, I use my client's Distraction Diary to determine the issues affecting my client's productivity health. You can use it this way, too. Begin by working directly in your notebook. Later, if you want to track your distractions electronically, check out tools like Toggl or RescueTime.

Worry

As we discussed earlier, many of us waste a lot of energy and time on worry. *What if I don't get done in time? Did I do that right? What if an asteroid hit the Earth today?* We might worry about hundreds of things over the course of a week, but guess what? Most of the things we worry about will never come to pass. That's because our worry is rarely focused on the present or on realistic outcomes. Worry generally projects us into the future, where we imagine hypothetical situations and fret about worst-case scenarios.

One of my clients was really worried about having to talk to a staff member about their work being lower quality lately. They were afraid the talk would turn into a huge blowup and feared the potential conflict. I helped my client work out the best way to talk to the staff member, how to approach the problem, and how to word everything. I also had them develop contingency plans in case the meeting did blow up. The next time I saw him, he told me the meeting had gone very well; the staff member agreed their work had been slipping and promised to do better. So the worry was a waste of energy, but the preparedness for the worst-case scenario helped him ease his worry going into the meeting.

To illustrate how pointless worry is, I want you to try this: Think back to one year ago today. Do you remember what you worried about on that exact day one year ago? Unless you had a loved one in the hospital on that day or some other major event took place, chances are you can't remember your worries a year later—and certainly five years from now you won't remember what you worried about today.

One hundred years from now, all your worries will be gone. Our everyday worries just don't matter as time passes. So why not let them go today? The next exercise will help you.

If your worries are about things like remembering a task that isn't on your list, have a system where you can easily record notes on tasks and ideas as they occur to you. A simple notebook you carry everywhere will suffice, or you can take notes or add tasks on your smartphone. This gets these things out of your head and into a system where they can be dealt with.

EXERCISE: Your Worry Diary

In the same way you kept a Distraction Diary in the previous exercise, open your Stop Wasting Time notebook and title a new page "Worry Diary."

Keeping your notebook close at hand, record every time you worry about something. Are you worried about finances? Worried you won't get a task done on time? Worried about what others think of you? Start with phrases like "I am worried about . . ." or "I am afraid that . . ." For each worry, record how long you worried about it and what level of stress it gave you on a scale from 1 (low) to 5 (high).

Set a task to return to your Worry Diary in one month. Look through the items you listed in your Worry Diary and highlight all the ones that never happened. You will soon see that almost all of your worrying, probably 95 percent, was just wasted attention and energy because the vast majority of the problems you worried about didn't come to pass.

Taking Brain Breaks

People who work 60 or 80 hours or more each week don't realize how badly they are burning themselves out. Yes, in some workplaces, this level of overwork is common and even celebrated. Many people proudly claim they are "workaholics," mistaking the label for a good thing when, like other "-aholics," they really need an intervention and a 12-step program. If you fall into this category, I encourage you to seek help. Most of us, though, don't routinely put in such long hours, but we still need to give our brains a break.

If you don't take regular brain breaks, your brain will decide to go on vacation all on its own and leave you behind. So your brain won't work well when you need it. We have only so much brain power and focus in a day. It is important to take short breaks throughout the day to keep your brain fresh and to take time off in evenings and on weekends to recharge. Think of it as running a marathon. You don't cross the finish line at a marathon and then immediately start a second marathon the same length. You need recovery time.

Here are some of my techniques for getting brain breaks and recovery time throughout my day and week:

- ➤ I work in 30-minute blocks (with a timer) and then take a 5-minute break at the end of each block.

- ➤ I "reset" myself between each project or task by closing all the old computer windows, browser tabs, and programs opened during the last task. I take a deep breath and shift my focus totally from the old task to the new one.

- ➤ I take my lunch breaks. At lunch, I take a brisk 20-minute walk—preferably outdoors.

- I go home on time. I don't think about work or take work home in the evenings.

- I choose hobbies that are unlike my work. Since I work all day in front of a computer, I have hobbies like creating driftwood art, disc golf, stargazing, playing Native American flute, badminton, and hiking. All are fun, physically active hobbies that totally give my mind a break from work and my eyes a break from computer screens.

- I take *all* my vacation time.

- I have low-tech days where I don't use the computer or Internet.

All of these give my brain a refreshing break. When I come back to work following a weekend or even on a weekday, I dive into my to-do list with a great deal of focus and energy. Taking some much-needed time provides me with an excellent break from brain-intensive work.

To implement a variation of my system, try this:

1. Using a timer, work in 30-minute blocks and take a 5-minute break when the timer goes off.

2. Reset yourself between tasks by closing all unneeded programs and tabs on your computer or putting away any physical items you no longer need.

3. Take your lunch break and fit in a 20-minute walk.

4. Go home when the workday is over. Don't work on evenings and weekends.

5. Cultivate hobbies that intrigue you.

6. Schedule and take vacations, go on date nights with a partner, or have "adventure" days.

7. Make one day a week a low-tech day.

Surveys estimate that up to 50 percent of Americans don't take all their allotted vacation time. A CNN report says that Americans gave up 705 million vacation days in 2017. Don't make this mistake. Use your vacation time to create amazing experiences, build lifelong memories, and recharge your batteries.

Week Three: Action Plan

Since week two, you have been creating your daily super-structure at the end of every day. Good job! Continue to do this daily, either in your notebook or in your app or software. Remember to look at your to-do list as a living document; it needs constant attention.

This week, you started keeping a Distraction Diary and Worry Diary. Use these tools throughout the week to keep bringing your awareness to what's stopping you from getting done what you need to get done so that you can work to eliminate those distractions using the strategies in this chapter.

For each item on your to-do list, use a countdown timer to be sure that you are getting in your allotted time on each task. Stop the timer if you are interrupted. That's a great time to jot down in your Distraction Diary what interrupted you. When the timer goes off, give your brain a short break before starting on the next task.

Also, using the strategies offered, get a handle on any cannibal tasks by breaking them down into smaller components that you can schedule into your to-do list so that they don't continue to eat up your time. This week, also be sure that you are scheduling time for play and creativity and for achieving both personal and career goals, one step at a time.

Takeaways

➤ Time is more valuable than money.

➤ There are many "time bandits" throughout the day that you need to eliminate or reduce.

➤ Worry uses up energy to no useful purpose.

➤ Willpower and discipline levels are limited and must be used strategically.

YOU LEARNED HOW:

➤ To identify distractions so you can reduce them

➤ To record your worries to learn how to let them go

➤ To use your peak time to accomplish your highest-priority and most difficult tasks

➤ To take brain breaks so you can be fresher for the tasks you need to accomplish

5

Week Four:
Focus Up!

Why Is It So Hard to Focus?

One of the reasons it is so hard to focus is evolution. Our brains are built to be able to quickly shift attention from one thing to another. Our early ancestors lived in dangerous environments, so continuously monitoring the environment around them for threats is how they survived long enough to have descendants—us. The unwary didn't last long enough to reproduce, so in a way, nature rewarded those who *didn't* focus for extended periods on one thing and become oblivious to their surroundings. So this continual monitoring of our environment is hard-wired into us; we are the survivors of many generations that have learned to constantly assess their environment for survival.

The ability to rapidly and frequently shift attention was a great quality for our ancestors to have, but it is less helpful in modern times, when most of us are not under constant physical threat. Rather, many tasks require our sustained focus for extended periods. Fortunately, our ancestors also needed to be able to focus. Think of the amount of focus and skill it took to quietly stalk game and wait for the right moment to strike. Or the incredible focus it took to make a tool from stone, one tiny flake at a time. So this ability to focus is *also* built into our brains— it's just not as predominant (or innately urgent) as our drive to shift our attention and monitor the environment. That doesn't mean you can't leverage the capacity to focus. Let's look at some ways we can tap into the brain's skills to improve our focus.

Single-Tasking (Again)

Your brain is incredibly powerful. Yes, *your* brain. I'm not talking about human brains in general. I am talking about your brain specifically—the one inside your head. Now, you might be thinking, *If my brain is so powerful, why can't I get things done? Why is it so hard for me to pay attention when I need to?*

One reason we struggle with focus is that we cripple our brains by not letting them work properly. Instead of fully focusing on the task at hand, we multitask and are also surrounded by distractions like e-mail and TV and electronic devices, all vying for our critical mental energy. Cluttered with extraneous tasks and information, our brains become like a bird whose wings have been clipped: They can't take full flight. By multitasking—"clipping" the brain's ability to focus fully on the task at hand—we let our brains soar at only a tiny fraction of their real potential.

The ability for us to multitask is itself a myth—it's not something our brains are built to do. "Multitasking" is a term that was originally applied to computers built to handle multiple processes at once—not a term that applies to how humans work. Computers don't think and don't have distractions; they have multiple core "brains" that allow them to multitask. Scientific studies have shown that human minds can't really multitask in the same ways that multicore computers do. Instead, when we multitask, we are placing quick bursts of micro-focus on one task, then jumping to the next. So it's not really multitasking at all. It's more like serial single-tasking. Our brains are built to focus on only one thing at a time. These tiny bursts of focus that occur when we try to multitask just aren't sustained enough to complete complex tasks.

By learning to stop multitasking and embracing single-tasking with laser focus, we give our brains a chance to soar. Here are some of the key steps to making the switch from multitasking to single-tasking.

1. **Plan first.** At this point in the book, you have already created several actions plans for the day ahead. It isn't an accident that I asked you to complete these exercises. By building an action plan for the next day with your tasks laid out in priority sequence, you already have a step-by-step plan in place. You don't need to spend time and energy deciding what to do—you already planned what to do the previous day and can focus on the very first task.

2. **Reduce distractions.** We have already discussed common distractions and how to minimize them. Make sure you apply these techniques every day. If you are in a

busy office environment that is full of distractions, try closing your door (if you have one) or wearing headphones. Another alternative is to set up a daily "power hour"—one hour a day where you have full focus with no distractions. If you can't do this at work, consider trying a "power hour" at a coffee shop or library. You will be amazed at what you can accomplish in one hour of uninterrupted time with a deep focus.

3. **Complete one task at a time.** If you have your action plan in place and have cut out as many distractions as you can, simply pick the top-priority task in the time block and work on it until it is complete, then move to the next one.

Focus Timer

I run a focus timer continuously while I work. A focus timer is a countdown timer that helps you make sure you are spending the required amount of time on a task or project. I use the countdown timer that comes with my smartphone. You can also download countdown timer apps, find website countdown timers, or pick up an inexpensive kitchen timer. Any of these will work as a personal focus timer. The countdown timer must allow for different time settings and have an alarm that goes off when the countdown is complete.

As mentioned, I work in 30-minute blocks of time with a 5-minute break afterward. This is a variation of the Pomodoro Technique (see page 56). Here is how my process works when moving from one project/task to the next:

1. **Close down old projects.** I close all programs, tabs, apps, e-mails, etc., that I had open related to the old project.

2. **Choose next priority task.** I pick the next highest-priority item on my action plan for that time block.

3. **Take deep breaths.** I take about three deep breaths. These breaths help me focus and let go of the old project so I'll be ready for the next one.

4. **Set focus timer.** I set the focus timer for a 30-minute countdown and begin.

5. **Work with full focus**. I work with full focus for the entire 30 minutes. If I am interrupted for any reason, I pause the focus timer and then start it again after the interruption. This way, I ensure I put the full 30 minutes of time into each project or task.

6. **Task complete.** If the task is complete before 30 minutes are up, I move to the second-priority task for the time block and so on. Many times I get multiple tasks completed within 30 minutes.

7. **Timer end.** When the alarm sounds, I turn it off and add notes to the task in my task management system as to where I left off so the next time I work on this task again I know exactly where to start.

8. **Repeat.** Then I repeat the process with the next task or time block.

Chunking (Batching Tasks) and Time Blocking

Working on tasks is more efficient when you work in chunks or batches. Here's what I mean by that: Imagine answering one e-mail, then returning a phone call, then spending five minutes writing a report, then jumping to another e-mail, and then repeating the process. This scattered approach and jumping around never lets you fully focus on anything, and your report would take forever to write using that method.

Instead, organize your schedule so that each type of task gets its own "chunk" of time, during which you're paying attention to that task alone. So in the example I just gave, instead of hopping around from e-mails to phone calls to the report, you could work for 30 minutes on e-mails, then 30 minutes on planning, then an hour on writing, and then spend a half hour returning phone calls.

This approach allows you to gain much deeper focus in your work, especially for areas that need more brainpower like planning and writing. Chunking also reduces the time it takes you to get up to speed on a new task. For example, if you are already responding to e-mails, the program is already open. You may have received different e-mails on the same subject, so your mind is already focused on that subject, and so on.

When you start a new task, it takes you a while to get fully into the new task. You have to decide how to approach it, the best way to complete it, etc. Think of it like a factory setting up for a run on a new product. The initial setup takes time, but once the start-up phase is done, the factory churns out the product quickly. Similarly, it's much faster for you to work on many similar tasks in a batch because you just have the one initial setup time. This is especially powerful when you have a number of small tasks that are similar.

Here are some common tasks that are easier to complete with batching:

- E-mails
- Phone calls
- Running errands (saves going out multiple times)
- Delegating
- Filing
- Reviewing job applications
- Reading
- Planning
- Training and learning

Take this concept a step further by having themed time blocks to move your batched tasks into. In my case, I have time blocks for:

- Marketing
- Product development
- Content development—blog articles, YouTube videos, infographics
- Workshop development
- Client projects
- Administration
- Personal development—learning new skills and honing existing skills

By having broad categories that my work falls into, I can make sure I spend enough time each week on each block. For example, I had a client who got so bogged down in his normal work that he couldn't work on the new product he was developing. He was running significantly behind schedule with an upcoming launch date.

I helped him set up the first two hours of his morning to only work on the new product and then have the rest of his work go into the rest of his day. I had him keep the new product time inviolate, telling his staff that they could only disturb him after 11:00 a.m. With this block of uninterrupted focus time dedicated to his product launch, he had no problem meeting his deadline. He also found that his regular work still got done in the time blocks he set aside for regular work. This is because tasks will expand to fill all your time blocks if you don't rein them in and restrict them to an amount of time appropriate to their importance.

The other benefit of these techniques is that by moving between different types of tasks, your brain is more engaged than if you tried to do the same tasks all day. This goes a long way in reducing the fatigue that often arises when we're focused on doing one thing for long periods. Rather than sitting down and writing this book all in one sitting, instead I had a block of time each day dedicated to writing. That way, I didn't get sick of writing the book, had more time for research, was able to incorporate more recent ideas triggered by working with clients, and had time for my mental back burner to suggest more ideas to include in the book.

Meditation: Breath Awareness

How do you reclaim your focus when there are multiple things happening around you all clamoring for your attention? You can start by learning to focus on just one thing—breathing. When was the last time you thought about your breathing? Unless you or a loved one have a respiratory problem, you likely never think about it. But when you can't breathe, everything else is unimportant. I watched my father slowly die over many years from emphysema, and I resolved never to take breathing for granted.

Have you ever watched a baby sleep? When a healthy baby breathes in, their belly expands. Babies breathe from the belly. We are meant to breathe using our belly as well. But when we are under stress, we tend to breath more shallowly—breathing from the chest instead of from our belly. Breathing from the chest tends to make our neck and shoulder muscles do more work, creating neck and shoulder tension, which can further interfere with our focus.

Becoming aware of your breath and breathing from your belly instead of your chest will have a huge impact on your ability to focus. When I am getting ready to speak on stage, I take several deep cleansing breaths, breathing with my belly to help me relax and clear my focus. I also take three deep breaths between projects to help let go of the former and focus on the next one.

Here is a meditation that will help you become more aware of your breathing. You can do this in front of a mirror if you want to make sure your belly is expanding rather than your chest while you breathe.

1. Stand up. Let your hands dangle loosely at your sides. Have a relaxed posture.

2. Breathe in through your nose for a slow count to four. Fully expand your belly as you take the breath. Try not to think about anything and just focus on your inhale.

3. Purse your lips slightly and breathe out through your mouth for a slow count of four.

4. Repeat this 10 times while focusing solely on your breathing.

By using this kind of mindful meditation to focus on your breath, you are now fully focused on one thing (your breath) and have let go of the other things distracting you. When you are fully focused on one thing (breathing), it is easier to transfer this focus to single-tasking instead of multitasking.

Meditation: Open Awareness

There are many forms of meditation, including mindful meditation and open awareness. Unlike mindful meditation where you focus on something like the breath (which you did in the previous exercise), open awareness is putting yourself into a relaxed state of awareness without a specific focus. Think of it as sitting under a wide sky on the prairie, being present in the moment, and letting your surroundings be what they are as you passively observe with a "wide-angle lens."

Don't try to judge, think about, or analyze the experience; just let it happen and flow through your awareness. I know this sounds weird, given that this chapter is all about focus. But letting go of focus during meditation gives your mind a chance to relax and reset, which increases your ability to focus later. To start, here is a simple exercise to try open awareness meditation by observing the sky:

1. Go outside and find a spot where you can be undisturbed. Turn off the notifications on your smartphone and tuck your phone away.

2. Stand or sit comfortably. Take a few deep breaths to release tension and calm your mind, and then just breathe naturally. Don't judge your breath or body sensations; allow them to be what they are.

3. Look up at the expansiveness of the sky with a soft gaze. Your mind is like the sky: open and expansive. Simply observe the sky without focusing on any one part of it. Take it all in without assigning any labels or judging it. In other words, be a passive observer.

4. As thoughts come into your mind, allow them to float away like the clouds. Like the clouds in the sky, thoughts come, pass across your awareness, and then exit your field of awareness. Just as the sky doesn't need to do anything with the clouds, your mind does not need to do anything with the thoughts.

5. Let the sounds and sights surround you without focusing your attention on any of it. Continue to passively observe whatever you feel, think, and see.

6. After 10 minutes or so, take a few deep breaths and then move on to your next task.

You can practice open awareness anywhere; you don't have to be under a big sky for it to work. By becoming more open and aware of your surroundings and sensations without assigning any thoughts or judgments to them, you are cleansing your mind, which frees you up to focus more fully on your next task. Open awareness also helps your mental back burner start simmering. Think of this type of meditation as a "computer reset button" for your brain, clearing out all the mental clutter and making room in your working brain for fuller attention and higher thinking.

The Mind-Body Connection

How does our mind-body connection affect focus? Have you ever tried to work with an excruciating toothache or a pounding headache? How many times have you dragged at work after a sleepless night or after a bout with the flu? Have you ever tried to get something done while your stomach was rumbling? How difficult was it to focus in these cases? Chances are you answered, "Impossible!" That's because our ability to focus is strongly tied to our physical body's feelings and rhythms—and when our body is suffering, *everything* we do suffers.

Pain, hunger, fatigue, and poor physical health all interfere with our ability to focus deeply, so we need to address these issues or take steps to avoid them. If we can't bring ourselves to deep focus levels, we procrastinate on the more difficult and complex tasks and work only on the easy ones. Any one or more of these focus-reducing factors may be contributing to your tendency to procrastinate.

Sleep

Let's start with our mind-body connection by talking about sleep. Adults require seven to nine hours a night to be fully rested. If we aren't fully rested, our brain doesn't function at its full potential. If you aren't able to sleep well at night, here are some suggestions to help you sleep better:

Go to bed earlier—in the dark. Our bodies have evolved for periods of light (when we are active) and dark (when we sleep and rest). With the creation of electric light, we now stay up later than our ancestors did and often don't give ourselves enough rest. The light triggers our bodies to stay awake later. So dim your lights in the evening, turn in earlier, and use room-darkening shades if possible.

Restrict screen time. Televisions, tablets, and smart-phones all have screens that are brightly lit, and the blue light they emit has been proven to keep us from falling into our normal sleeping cycle. To combat this, stop watching or using any screens, including your TV, computer, tablet, or smartphone, an hour or two before sleep. If this isn't possible, at least turn down the brightness on your screens. There are computer and smartphone apps that can dim your screen at night. I love to read just before I go to bed, so I use an e-ink screen (like you get with a Kindle) with a variable brightness option that I turn way down for e-book reading at night.

Check mattresses and pillows. Is your bed comfortable? How about your pillows? It surprises me that people are generally more willing to spend money on comfortable couches than they are on better beds when we spend so much of our lives in our beds. While I am frugal by nature, I happily spend more on a bed, pillows, and comforters that help me sleep better. If you have an uncomfortable mattress or pillows, consider replacing them.

Create a comfortable sleeping temperature. It is nearly impossible to sleep if you are too cold or too hot. It is worth spending the extra money on air-conditioning for your bedroom if you get hot or on better bedding, quilts, or electric blankets if you get cold. Make sure you have the tools you need to create a comfortable sleeping temperature for yourself. You can also control temperature through the sleepwear you choose. Save the sexy sleepwear for special occasions and choose comfortable sleepwear that doesn't constrict you and that is the right weight for your room temperature.

Avoid food and alcohol before bed. Large amounts of alcohol have been shown to negatively affect sleep patterns and can cause you to make multiple trips to the bathroom at night. Eating food late at night makes your digestive system work harder, which can keep you awake.

If none of these suggestions help you get a better night's sleep, consider going to a sleep clinic. A sleep clinic will check for any medical problems that might be affecting your sleep. You can also speak with your doctor for advice. Your ability to focus should improve when you are more well rested.

Eat

Food is fuel! Human beings need plenty of fuel, and the right kind, to keep our minds working at maximum effectiveness. Our brains use more energy than our other organs. In fact, it uses up to 20 percent of the body's total energy load. To run our large brains at high efficiency, we need good fuel. What is "good" fuel for our brains, and how do we make sure we get this good food? Here are some foods that have been shown to help brain function:

- Avocados
- Blueberries
- Broccoli
- Eggs
- Nuts and seeds
- Oranges and other vitamin C–rich foods
- Pumpkin
- Trout and sardines
- Turmeric
- Wild salmon

In addition to feeding our brains, we also need to be cautious about the negative effects of some food. These foods have been shown to be harmful to brain function:

- Alcohol (in excess)
- Aspartame

- Highly processed foods
- Sugary drinks like soda, sports drinks, energy drinks, and fruit juice

What about caffeine? Studies have shown that a moderate amount of caffeine, like what you get from coffee and tea, is perfectly fine and does give you a lift. But drinking coffee all day is beyond the moderate amount and causes you to crash late in the afternoon. When I was a regular coffee drinker, I would go through a large pot per day, easily. About 3:00 p.m., I would have a spectacular "caffeine crash" where I had no energy left to work on anything. So now I just drink coffee in the morning and restrict myself to two cups. I recommend you try to stick to one or two cups of coffee or tea per day. Some types of coffee have more caffeine than others so check the caffeine levels listed on the package.

Be aware that energy drinks have up to eight times more caffeine than coffee; even a single energy drink may be above the recommended caffeine limit per day. These energy drinks can be dangerous and have been associated with increased anxiety, headaches, migraines, insomnia, high blood pressure, and heart attacks. I suggest you avoid energy drinks or, if you must use them, restrict yourself to one per day.

Move

Your body wants to move! It wasn't built to spend all day working in front of a computer and all evening sitting on a couch watching TV. But you already knew that, didn't you? Still, you might be tempted to skip the exercise after a long day of accomplishing the tasks on your to-do list. I've been there.

I used to schedule a weekly evening game of badminton with my brother and some friends at a local gymnasium. Some nights I was so mentally tired from work that I really didn't feel like going. But I didn't want to be the one to wuss out and let my friends down. (A big score for accountability buddies!) So I would drag myself out and start playing. Once I got into the game, I really enjoyed it and was glad I went out. At the end, I felt physically tired, but I could feel that my body was really happy that I'd had the physical activity—and my brain felt more awake than it had before the game.

If you need a reason to stop procrastinating and get moving, consider these benefits for your brain and ability to focus:

More oxygen: During exercise, your heart rate increases, pumping more oxygen into your brain. Oxygen is critical to brain growth and healing, and the brain uses about three times as much oxygen as your muscles do. Watching my father struggling with dementia when his brain was oxygen-starved due to emphysema really hit home to me how important it is to keep a steady flow of oxygen to the brain.

Hormones and neurotransmitters: During exercise, your body releases hormones and other chemicals that help your brain work better, including neurotransmitters to boost brain activity and improve mood.

Better memory: Just 120 minutes of moderate exercise a week has been shown to improve memory.

Wake-up call: Exercising is a wake-up call to your brain. Since your body is more active, the brain perks up to deal with the extra activity. This is why a walk at lunchtime is great for helping you focus in the afternoon.

To increase your ability to focus (and make your body happy), schedule some exercise into your daily routine. This could be a morning workout, a walk at lunch, an evening swim, or virtually any other physical activity. It also helps to take regular stretch breaks throughout the day.

If you don't think you have the discipline to start and maintain an exercise program on your own, you can try:

- Exercising with a friend and keeping each other accountable
- Signing up for fitness classes
- Working with a personal trainer
- Joining a sports team

Take it easy when you start a new exercise program, especially if you have been sedentary, as overdoing physical activity can be damaging to your body. Consult a doctor if you are out of shape or have medical issues that might impact your starting an exercise program or playing a sport.

EXERCISE: How Are You Feeling Right Now?

In your Stop Wasting Time notebook, title a new page
"How Is My Body Feeling Right Now?"

Now stand up and very slowly and deliberately stretch
your arms and legs one at a time. Feel the interplay of
muscles and the sensation of each stretch. Notice that
you probably weren't really paying attention to your body
until I asked you to stretch. This kind of check-in with your
body is important.

Close your eyes and feel each part of your body sep-
arately. Focus your attention on the shoulder of one arm,
then move down to your upper arm, forearm, wrist, and
fingers. Slowly move each part as you bring it to mind. Then
move on to your other arm, then legs, then up through your
torso, and to your neck and head. Move each part as you
move your attention through it.

In your notebook, write down what you have learned.
How are you feeling? If there is pain, where is it? Are you
feeling hungry or tired? What is your mood? This is all
important information that your body is sharing with you.
When you address your body's needs, you will find your
ability to focus improving.

Red Alert

On shows like *Star Trek*, the captain shouts, "Red alert!"
in emergency situations to call the crew to their battle
stations. There are flashing red lights and a loud, blaring

alarm to make sure everyone knows there is a serious problem that requires immediate attention.

Most of us have our own little red alert devices in our pockets or purses. Our smartphones sound continual alerts when we have new texts, e-mails, social media posts, and messages. And, yes, some people even use alert sounds from *Star Trek* for these notifications. But are these really red alert emergencies? Did we need to drop everything we were doing to check out the alert notification, losing our focus on the task at hand? Unless you are an on-call doctor or volunteer firefighter, chances are the notification was actually low priority and not worthy of red alert status. So how do we separate critical notifications from everyday messaging?

E-mail Alerts

Let's face it. The vast majority of your e-mail isn't that important. Newsletters, nonessential information, your friend's latest blog post, jokes, and even questions from clients and others are not always the most urgent tasks you should be focusing on.

I turn off my e-mail notifications entirely. Instead of an alert interrupting me, I check my e-mails on a regular basis at preset times. For me, it is twice a day, but maybe for you it is once every hour. With my notifications off, I am not interrupted every time a newsletter or some spam e-mail comes in. Because I do check and reply to my e-mail regularly, all my e-mail is still answered within one business day, so my clients are all taken care of and they don't even notice that I am only checking my e-mail periodically.

Turn off your e-mail alerts and set aside a time that works for you to check your e-mail, then sort or respond to them as needed (see page 61).

Calendar Alerts

Calendar alerts are one type of alert I *do* find useful. I set calendar alerts for time-specific things like client coaching sessions, doctor appointments, and events I want to attend. Because these events are attached to a certain date and time, they are worth having an alert for. I set the notification for a reasonable time ahead of the event—10 minutes ahead for a web-conferencing meeting or 45 minutes ahead for an appointment I need to travel to.

I don't have alerts for tasks that are due on a certain day. If I had 10 tasks due that day, that would be an additional 10 notifications from my calendar. Instead, I just check my task list daily to find all the tasks for that day and work on them.

Do set calendar alerts for time-based appointments but turn off task notifications.

Other Software and Media

People who run our software and smartphone apps all want us to think their notifications are the most important things in our day. Facebook and other social media apps, weather apps, game apps, and more all send out a deluge of notifications—if you let them. Almost none of these are worthy of a red alert interruption of your focus. Learn how to turn off these notifications on your phone and schedule regular times into your day when you check things like Facebook to see what is new.

Turn off software and app alerts and notifications, and set aside a time in your day to check in on what's going on.

Week Four: Action Plan

As you have now been doing each day, create your schedule for tomorrow either in your notebook, app, or software. Start batching your tasks into related categories so that you can accomplish similar tasks in the same time block. Knowing how your body's needs can interfere with your ability to focus and feel your healthiest, schedule in time for meditation, exercise, and proper nutrition. Also, do your best to reduce any interruptions from electronic notifications. Keeping all of this in mind, tomorrow's to-do list might look something like this:

➤ Planning
  - Turn all notifications off on my smartphone.
  - Turn off e-mail alerts.
  - Set a calendar alert for screen time cut off at 8:00 p.m.
  - Schedule 10 minutes of meditation at the start and/or end of day.
  - Schedule a 20-minute walk at lunch.

- Mind/Body
  - Shop for a new mattress.
  - Assess existing bedding and sleepwear for comfort and temperature control.
- Work Project
  - Task 1
  - Task 2
  - Task 3
- Personal Project
  - Task 1
  - Task 2
  - Task 3

Takeaways

➤ Our brains aren't built to multitask.

➤ Multitasking decreases efficiency by reducing focus.

➤ Chunking and batching tasks is more efficient than working on scattered tasks.

➤ The body affects the mind's ability to focus.

➤ Unnecessary notifications are like false red alerts, destroying our focus.

YOU LEARNED HOW:

➤ To improve focus by getting enough sleep, eating better, and moving more

➤ To reduce interruptions from notifications

➤ To single-task to improve focus

➤ To batch similar tasks together to improve efficiency

➤ To become more in tune with your body's needs

6

Week Five:
Keep Motivated

What's Your Motivation?

Many of my clients eagerly embrace the new tools and techniques I teach them, but then they struggle with how to keep using them over the long term. Even when they tell me the new techniques are having a major impact on their ability to get things done, there is still a tendency to fall back into old habits. Anyone who has tried to diet or quit smoking can relate to how hard it is to change habits that have been developed over many years.

The first step to pursuing personal change is identifying your reason for making the change. Usually your motivation is tied to the outcomes you are trying to attain. Ask yourself, *What is the outcome I want to achieve?* By connecting more deeply to why you want to stop procrastinating on something, you *can* find the motivation to succeed.

Let's say you've been putting off guitar lessons but really want to learn to play guitar. What is your desired outcome? To write songs, to perform onstage, to play simple songs for your kids? By visualizing a powerful outcome, one that you are passionate about, your motivation to devote your time to the task increases. Then it becomes a matter of setting up a regular block of time, accessing learning resources, and putting the time in. Remember the old adage "Slow and steady wins the race." Dedicated time is the secret to learning new things, finishing projects, and making meaningful changes.

Sustaining Motivation

At some point, you might get frustrated with your lack of progress and slack off. Then your dream of playing guitar, writing a book, cleaning the garage, finishing that report, or learning another language turns to dust. However, by keeping the outcome firmly in mind, you are constantly reminded of what is motivating this action. What is your reason for wanting to clean the garage? So your car can fit inside and won't sit out in the snow all winter? By visualizing your car safe and snug in your clean garage during the next snowstorm, you have a powerful motivator to get the work done.

You may be rolling your eyes right now and thinking, *Sure, Garland. That might work for a personal passion of mine or household improvements, but my problem is procrastinating when I have to do something boring, like my work!* So how do you sustain motivation when you are faced with a boring task or a job you aren't passionate about? Here are some ways to stay motivated even when you are doing something you would rather not do because it bores you to tears:

Remember your "why." For example, if you aren't passionate about your work, learn to take joy in the fact that your work lets you take care of yourself and your family and provides funds toward your hobbies and travel. Without your work, you would have none of this. (Revisit the exercise on page 34.)

Find small pleasures. At work, find some small parts you do enjoy and save them as a reward for after you finish the boring, unmotivating parts. At home, a sink full of dirty dishes may be your chance to listen to your favorite music.

Create your own rewards (gamify). If you have a very boring task to get through, come up with your own reward system to turn your productivity progress into a game. This can be as simple as awarding yourself a gold star for completing something or rewarding yourself with a small luxury purchase or activity once you complete the task. Think of it as a game to complete as many tasks and collect as many gold stars as you can. You can connect these gold stars to real rewards if you choose.

Fake it till you make it. Strangely, studies have proven that pretending to be happy by smiling actually does make you happier. Somehow our body and brain get tricked into going along with it and our mood becomes happier. Similarly, fake motivation until it becomes part of your process.

Use a boring job as a stepping-stone. If you dislike your job, think of it as a stepping-stone to the next stage of your career. Treat your existing work as something you need to become exceptional at so that you can "level up" later. The skills you hone in your existing job may be critical as your career improves and your responsibilities increase. You can also take courses and network to help you move toward a career you are more passionate about.

Task Values Reflection

Connecting the importance of a task to your values can motivate you to stop procrastinating on it. So think about a long-term task, one that is important to you but that you have been putting off getting to. In your Stop Wasting Time notebook, title a new page with the name of the task. Under the task, list in bullet point form how the task aligns with your values. Why is it important to you? The value is not a concrete goal you achieve and then you're done—although goals can be very motivating, too!. It is something you want your life to be about. The task can be anything you've been procrastinating on, but here are two examples of connecting to values and goals:

Example 1

Task: Start fitness program

Values:
- Have energy
- Take care of my family

- Participate in activities I enjoy
- Maintain long-term health and remain active as I get older

Example 2

Task: Set up a recurring savings plan of $200 per month

Goals:
- Be frugal in everyday purchases
- Have a reserve fund for emergencies
- Have a savings account for vacations and special experiences

Now that you have a task you have been procrastinating on and have examined how it aligns with your values, make sure the first step in the task is scheduled for the soonest possible day and that you set aside a time block for it.

Subdivisions

Sometimes a large task or project just feels too big to take on, so we put the big project off until some undetermined time in the future when we might have more time. For example, let's say you have an idea for a new product that would take 160 hours to develop (four weeks at 40 hours a week). The problem is that you will unlikely have this large block of unoccupied time (a whole month) where you could ignore your daily work to take on a project of this size. The only way to complete a larger project like this is to subdivide it into smaller chunks that you can work on. The first few tasks to start on might look like this:

1. Concept: Write new product concept document.

2. Market research: Do some preliminary research to see if there is a market for it.

3. Development plan: Put together a development plan to create the product.

4. Marketing plan: Work on marketing plan ideas to promote the product.

Here is another example: Let's say you want to earn your master's degree. A worthy goal, but how to get started? A master's degree takes years of work. When the task is subdivided, we might end up with a starting task list like this:

1. **Research fields:** Investigate which career fields are growing and likely to pay well in 10 years that also connect to your interests and skills.

2. **Choose degree:** Determine the type of university degree that will be most likely to help you gain employment in the field you chose.

3. **Choose university:** Research universities to find out which ones offer the best degree programs in your chosen field.

4. **Funding:** Research funding possibilities like student loans, scholarships, and savings programs.

5. **Entry requirements:** Do you have the correct academic entry requirements? If not, you can start by taking courses to upgrade your transcript.

As you can see, we have now broken down a daunting four- to seven-year project into some starting tasks you can begin today or this week. This works for any large project. Even something as large as constructing a house can begin with:

1. Researching neighborhoods

2. Researching builders

3. Checking mortgage and finance options

4. Reviewing floor plans

If you have a large project you have been putting off, start subdividing it and breaking it down into smaller, more manageable chunks that can be handled one task at a time.

One-Day Resolutions

Ever make major life-changing resolutions at New Year's only to have them fail a few months later? Yeah, me too. Grand resolutions seem like such a great idea but usually fail miserably for most of us. We *are* more likely to complete something we're committed to, but big changes are more difficult to implement than small ones.

Instead of a yearly resolution, consider making a very short-term resolution to act on—a one-day resolution. So, for example, let's say your major commitment is to get more fit. This is a big task, and there are so many different ways you could go about it. A one-day commitment might be to do just one thing today that will make a difference. Today's one-day commitment might be to take a walk at lunch or to get up a half hour early to do a short yoga routine. Then you could expand that out to the next day and so on. After about three weeks, your new commitment becomes a habit, one day at a time.

The next level of this major commitment might be to sign up at a fitness center. The day after that, you might choose three days in your schedule where you go to the fitness center for one to two hours. Your resolution on the first day of this schedule would be to keep the scheduled fitness appointment, and so on. Now you are getting a walk at lunch every day plus three fitness center visits a week. And you did it in very small, short, one-day commitments.

If you put these commitments in writing, you are more likely to keep them, so write your one-day resolution down and schedule it in your time block or calendar. Set a notification on your smartphone to go off when it is time to get ready for your walk or go to the fitness center. This is an allowable use of "red alerts."

It also helps to tell someone that you've made a commitment to do something. We are more likely to follow through when the people around us know about our commitments and support us. Plus, we feel silly when we announce our new goals to others and don't follow through, so there is some added incentive for us to stick to our resolution. (See "Buddy Up!" on page 145.)

Do the Worst Thing First

Earlier I discussed that willpower and discipline are limited, so you want to use them wisely. The best way to use these limited resources is to do the worst thing you have to do *before* you do *anything* else. Do this by setting a timer and working on the task you have identified for one or two 30-minute blocks and work with full focus. I find it easier to handle a distasteful project if I know I only have to work on it for the first half hour or hour of the day. Then you can reward yourself after the worst task with an easier, more enjoyable task. But *only* after you have put in your block of time on your worst tasks.

This also applies to any large, difficult project. Dedicate the first hour or so of your day to working on it, and you will be surprised by how much easier it gets. With focused time spent every day on the worst tasks, you will eventually find that even the largest and most complex projects are completed more quickly.

Plan Your Day around Your Commitment

Now that you have made your commitments for one-day resolutions and your "worst first" projects, you need to plan your day around them. Keep your first block of time for the worst tasks, but also have time blocks set up for your other important commitments.

Whether it is fitness, learning a musical instrument, taking a course, or writing a book, you need to have a scheduled block of time for these in your week. This time *must* be kept sacred. Don't let work, other people, or other happenings intrude on this sacred time. If friends want to do things with you during your scheduled time, tell them you are tied up for those hours and suggest several other blocks of time that would work for you.

Being persistent with your time-block scheduling will let you achieve things you have wanted to do for years but have always eluded you. *Only* by dedicating these time blocks can you succeed in your goals.

Reward Yourself

As I touched upon earlier, we work better when we feel we are rewarded for our efforts. It's nice when the reward comes from our boss in the form of a pat on the back or a raise or when a partner thanks us with a special gift for getting the garage cleared of junk, but we aren't usually in control of that part. So it helps to set up your own reward system. Rewards don't have to be something of great value—just something that *feels* like a reward. Here are some inexpensive, easy ways to create rewards for yourself:

Crossing tasks off: Some people get great joy from physically crossing tasks off their list. You can make a big production of this. Have a special ruler and marker you use for crossing tasks off your to-do list and relish banishing that task from your day.

Gold stars: You can also give yourself a gold star whenever you successfully complete a task or a focused activity. For example, you could give yourself a star whenever you manage to work for a 30-minute uninterrupted block or whenever you remember to work on the top-priority item instead of being distracted. (This system also works great for kids when you let the gold stars build toward a toy or experience they want.)

Don't break the chain: To make sure he wrote new material every day, comedian Jerry Seinfeld put a calendar on his wall and drew a big red X on the days when he accomplished the task. He found the process rewarding, and the growing chain of red X's motivated him to keep writing every day so he wouldn't have to break the chain. Similarly, you can make a chain of red X's by knocking out good productivity activities such as setting your next day's to-do list in priority sequence or working on your worst task first. If you do this every day, you will create a motivating habit to do that activity and keep your chain unbroken.

Activities/small luxuries: You can reward yourself if you meet your daily goals by splurging on a personal activity you enjoy or a minor luxury. For me, I might treat myself to an archery outing, a new golf disc (more fun and less expensive than regular golf), or a new shaving brush. You can combine this with the gold star program and work toward accumulating gold stars to earn other rewards.

LARGER REWARDS

Adding up: You can add incentives to maintaining your calendar chain or collecting gold stars by establishing additional reward levels as they add up. For example, you could have special rewards for chains of 30, 60, or 90 days. One person I knew quit smoking this way. Every day he didn't smoke, he put aside a dollar amount equivalent to what he spent on his habit into an account to save for a new all-terrain vehicle. As his savings grew, he had great incentive to continue to avoid smoking. He would envision all the fun he would have on his new vehicle out in the woods with his friends.

Meeting large goals: If you meet a large goal, you can reward yourself with activities or things that match the goal's importance. Buying a new car because you got one priority task done is probably overboard, but you can have a sliding scale that might include:

- A nice dinner out at a new restaurant you've being wanting to try
- An art class or photography workshop
- New headphones
- A cabin retreat weekend
- A tropical vacation

You don't have to wait for others to reward you. Set up your own reward system that works for you and link these rewards to completing tasks that help you achieve your professional and personal goals.

Ask Yourself "Why?"

As I've mentioned, "Why?" is one of the most important questions you can ask yourself. *Why am I doing this? Why does this task need to get done? Why is this task a priority?* "Why" gives the everyday tasks you do meaning. When you know why a task is important—that is, how it connects with your values or goals—you have more motivation to see it through to completion. If you look hard enough, you can always find some reason you care about what you're doing, even if it's the most mundane part of your day.

Finding Your Everyday Inspiration

You aren't just plodding along for no reason. For example, you work to earn a living to support yourself and/or your family because you value a happy, healthy family; you do household chores to keep your home in good shape because you value a clean and orderly living space; you exercise regularly because you value staying healthy, and so on. Keep these reasons in your awareness every day to remain inspired to embrace the task in front of you, even when what you are doing isn't exciting.

You can also look for some small aspect of your task that aligns with your values to keep you inspired. I have always valued good customer service, for example, so even when I worked in a job I didn't care for, I would light up whenever a customer came in or called because I really love helping people. It also made my day go more quickly. Helping customers became my everyday inspiration.

At home, your everyday inspiration may be something as simple as the wonderful feeling you get when you slip into a bed with freshly laundered sheets because you value comfort, or how your body feels after eating a healthy dinner because you value health. Maybe it is how your family lights up when you play the guitar, because you value having a happy family.

In your Stop Wasting Time notebook, title a new page "My Everyday Inspiration." Think about all the tasks you need to do on a daily basis, especially the ones you don't necessarily enjoy. Then, spend a few moments thinking about why you are doing each task and how it aligns with your values. Create simple bullet points as you did in the exercise on page 34. The difference between these two exercises is that now you are looking at your daily, everyday tasks instead of a long-term undertaking.

Buddy Up!

Many of my clients feel they are more productive when they work with me because our weekly coaching session keeps them accountable, which helps them stay focused on what they want to accomplish. But not everyone has the budget to work with a professional time management coach. If you fall into that category, but you still want to be accountable to someone because you think it will help you stay on track, get an accountability buddy. This can be a friend, colleague, family member, or other person you team up with to hold each other accountable for doing what you each set out to do.

The idea is to share your weekly goals with your buddy and then schedule a weekly talk to discuss the progress each of you made toward your goals. Your buddy is your cheerleader, encouraging you to stay on track, and you are theirs. Just knowing you have to tell your buddy the results of your efforts each week will help you stay motivated to accomplish your tasks. Also, brainstorming your issues with your buddy can help you over a hump, provide a new perspective, or reveal new ways to succeed.

If you would like to work with me directly to help keep you accountable, visit CaptainTime.com and click on the coaching options.

Staying on Track
When It All Goes Wrong

You are faced with a "crisis" situation: Your plan for the day got shot all to heck, the phone keeps ringing, and the e-mails are pouring in. Now what? How do you keep on track when all you are doing is putting out fires? In addition to the advice to follow, here are three steps to get you back on track quickly:

1. **Don't beat yourself up.** It happened; now just deal with it. The energy you waste on being upset that your plans have been derailed is better spent solving the problem.

2. **Re-triage.** You originally triaged your tasks to assign priorities, but you now have a full set of new tasks to incorporate into your day. So now it is time to do triage again. You need to quickly assess the priority levels of the new tasks and see where they fit in among your existing tasks. Some apps let you drag and drop your tasks into priority sequence to reorder them. This is a very fast way to reorganize tasks by priority. (See page 70 for a discussion on prioritizing your to-do list.)

3. **Set micro time blocks.** Maybe you normally work in 30-minute blocks, but now that your day is derailed, you have less time to devote to each task. Instead, do a quick 10- to 15-minute assessment of each task. Find the highest-priority tasks, identify blockages in the flow, delegate what you can to those who can help *before* working on your highest-priority tasks, and get those projects moving. If possible, treat your tasks like a carousel, rotating through each one and spending just 15 minutes on each until you feel you have a handle on everything. Then, the next day, revert to your standard-length time blocks.

Stick to the Essentials

Ever notice how you seem to get a lot more done just before you go on a vacation? This is because you are ignoring long-term work and just focusing on the essentials that need to be completed before you go away. Similarly, when everything is off track, you need to get back to the essentials and ignore the long-term work temporarily. Narrow your focus to the highest-priority, urgent tasks and make sure they are delegated or worked on. But don't let this narrow focus become an everyday occurrence, as never working on the open and long-term projects will come back to bite you later.

On the Fly

I love to plan, but I hate it when other circumstances mess up my plan. Whatever the reason, I have a strong internal resistance to changing my plans. When something happens to screw up my schedule, I find myself trying to just do minor adjustments instead of making a new plan reflecting the new circumstances. While persistence is important in many cases, it can cross the line into stubbornness if you aren't careful.

Look at what messed up your plans. Is it best to adapt your plan or just to create a new plan on the fly? If there are major changes to your situation, you are usually better off changing your perspective and developing a new plan to fit the new circumstances. Don't face new situations based on old thinking.

Ask for Help

During your triage, you may notice that there is no way to actually get a task done in the time needed. In this case, request help from others. At work, some people or places to get help from include managers, subordinates, coworkers, mentors, virtual assistants and other freelancers, online discussion forums, and support lines. At home, you can turn to family, friends, handymen and other paid workers, and so on. We are often slow to admit we need help and want to go it alone, but it doesn't hurt to ask for help.

In business, it is your manager's job to assist you in exceptional circumstances. In addition to managers and coworkers, you can also outsource part of the work to freelancers or virtual assistants if you are able to hire them. Of course, if want to hire outside people for things like data entry or graphic design or anything proprietary for your company, you'll probably need to seek permission.

Outsourcing is especially useful for things like Internet research. For example, if you have been tasked to find the best software solution for one of your company's problems but you have some fires to put out, you could outsource this task and then develop your own recommendations based on the research prepared by your virtual assistant when things calm down again. It is much faster to complete a report after someone else has done the time-consuming research. In this case, no one inside your company even needs to know you have help. (Many successful people hire virtual assistants to help with a variety of tasks like Internet research, personal scheduling, planning travel, and more.)

When facing difficulties concerning a software program, which can happen both at home and the office and derail the whole day, I make full use of the software support that comes with the program. After all, the support people are experts on their software and can likely point me to a solution that might have taken me hours to find on my own in a few minutes. I also find online discussion forums to be fantastic resources. Posting a question in one of these forums on virtually any topic usually gives me a harvest of ideas in just a few hours or a few days at most.

Week Five: Action Plan

As you've been doing, create your schedule for tomorrow either in your notebook, app, or software. This time make a note of your motivations for each task so you can keep *why* they are important in mind. You don't have to do this every time you create your to-do list, but if you are ever unsure about why you are doing something, it helps to remind yourself. So at least for tomorrow's superstructure, make an effort to find a "why" for each item.

As you start putting together tomorrow's schedule, keep the following in mind:

> Take care of the "worst first" to make sure your most difficult tasks and projects get attention during your peak focus time.

> Break larger projects into smaller modules and tasks.

> Schedule an action to keep your one-day resolution.

Look over each action plan from the previous weeks. You should now have a solid system in place to continue creating a superstructure for the next day that's based on your preferences and what works best for you. Nice going!

Takeaways

YOU LEARNED THAT:

➤ Motivation can be sustained by connecting to the "why" of the task.

➤ Having a reward system helps you stay motivated during boring tasks.

➤ Short-term commitments are easier to keep than large, life-changing ones, but they will eventually lead to big change.

YOU LEARNED HOW:

➤ To do the worst task first

➤ To use an accountability buddy to help you keep your commitments

➤ To get back on track when everything goes wrong

7

Your Road to Success

Congratulations!

Congratulations! You've come a long way in our five weeks together. You've explored the roots of your procrastination, and you've learned skills, strategies, and techniques to stop wasting time and start getting things done. You have everything you need to end your cycle of procrastination. But, in my experience, many people struggle to keep their early success going, so let's address this now.

Think of this book as an ongoing resource. You can reread this book from time to time to refresh yourself on these techniques, and get back on track when you falter. You can also follow my blog at CaptainTime.com to learn about new techniques and resources. In addition to rereading the book, let's explore some other ideas on how to make sure your long-term success.

Find the Best Process for You

When people ask me which of the time management programs I follow, the answer is none and all of them. There is no one time management system to "rule them all" that works for everyone, because everyone works differently. My wife and I use different apps and approaches, but we are both very productive. The reason my wife uses different apps and approaches is that she has a different learning style than I do.

Instead of committing to one system and following its singular approach dogmatically, I "borrow" the best tactics and strategies from each system I encounter. I recommend you take the same approach. I think of learning time management as exploring, applying, and adapting what you learn to apply it to your own situation rather than adopting a singular system. Fully test each of the techniques and strategies in this book and see which ones resonate with you and work best in your particular situation. Commit to using these techniques faithfully on a daily basis and expand upon them.

If there is a technique I suggest that just doesn't seem to work for you, look at the problem this technique is meant to solve. Do you actually *have* that problem? If not, you can shelve the technique until you need it. If you have that problem, but the technique doesn't solve it, modify the technique to suit your needs or look for additional techniques and try them out until you find one that solves the problem *and* works for you. You may also find that you don't need some of the techniques right now, but those techniques may become important as your responsibility grows or as some of the simpler procrastination problems are solved.

Tune-Ups and Check-Ins

It is important to continually revisit your productivity systems to make sure they are working for you. You can do this independently or in conjunction with your accountability buddy or coach. Don't get complacent even if things are going well. Continually check in and ask yourself:

- Is this the next-most-important task to undertake?
- Is there a better way to do this?
- Could this task be automated?
- Can I delegate this task to someone else or outsource it?
- Do I have time set aside this week for each personal and career goal?

Remember to seek out help when you need it. This can be from your team, your manager, your accountability buddy, virtual assistants, freelancers, your family, your friends, paid helpers, or a time coach like me.

Be Your Own Best Ally

Learn to be your own best ally. Being kind to ourselves is one of the hardest lessons we have to learn. It is incredibly hard to succeed when your inner voice is continually criticizing you and destroying your confidence. Shut down your inner critic whenever it starts chirping at you. Take the time and energy you used to spend worrying and criticizing yourself and reinvest that time and energy into solving problems, learning more, and building yourself up.

If you are struggling with confidence, consider working with a coach or taking confidence-building courses online or in person. As you gain confidence, it shows and gains its own momentum. The more confident you feel, the more success you gain and the more you attract. As I gained confidence while speaking and teaching, more and more people started approaching me to speak at their events or to teach their teams. Now I am at the point where people find and approach me regularly and success comes much more easily.

When I face large projects and overwhelming workloads, I am confident that I have the skills to manage them superbly. Instead of worrying about the tasks ahead of me, I am like an emergency room professional—triaging the tasks, assigning priorities, and ensuring critical tasks are taken care of first. Don't get me wrong—I still find some tasks distasteful or boring, but I have strategies to deal with them (if I can't delegate or outsource them) instead of putting them off. And I have shared those strategies with you.

Don't Forget Your Personal Life

While many of the examples and techniques I've talked about in this book are especially useful for ending procrastination at work, don't forget to give your personal life some TLC as well. Our personal goals and dreams are in many ways *more* important than work ones, but somehow, we always put work first and put off our personal goals. To give yourself the TLC you deserve, set aside weekly blocks of time for working on your personal goals, hobbies, and passions and keep this time inviolate. Don't let work or other people overwrite this key sacred time.

Do It for *You*

We are not really taught to value ourselves. We are told it is selfish to take care of ourselves and that we should we focus on our family and others. Even our work makes us feel selfish when we take care of our own needs. But, by taking care of ourselves first, we now have the energy, time, skills, and success to take care of others, whether it is just our own family, our colleagues, our local community, or our work. Perhaps you will even take care of your country by running for a government office. When you are elected, or as your success grows, let me know how adopting the procrastination techniques in this book helped you get there.

Procrastinator's Checklist

Use the following checklist to make sure you followed all the steps needed to stop wasting time and start getting things done:

- [ ] **Awareness (Week 1)**
  - [ ] Become aware and mindful of when you procrastinate
  - [ ] Find the root of your procrastination on each task using the Downward Arrow technique
  - [ ] Replace negative thoughts with positive thoughts
- [ ] **Superstructure (Week 2)**
  - [ ] Get a task list system in place, either written, app-based, or software-based
  - [ ] Triage tasks and set priorities
  - [ ] Use the Zero E-mail Inbox technique
  - [ ] Continuously recheck to make sure you are following system and priorities
  - [ ] Create your superstructure each day for the day ahead
- [ ] **Time Bandits (Week 3)**
  - [ ] Corral time bandits and minimize distractions
  - [ ] Schedule and take regular brain breaks

☐ **Focus (Week 4)**

    ☐ Implement single-tasking

    ☐ Minimize red alerts and notifications

    ☐ Chunk and batch tasks

    ☐ Meditate for focus and open awareness

    ☐ Establish good sleep habits

    ☐ Eat for peak energy

    ☐ Get regular exercise and movement

☐ **Motivation (Week 5)**

    ☐ Connect to why you do what you do

    ☐ Find motivation in everyday tasks

    ☐ Subdivide large or long projects

    ☐ Make one-day resolutions

    ☐ Schedule time blocks for your commitments

    ☐ Continuously recheck yourself by asking *"Why?"*

    ☐ Get an accountability buddy

    ☐ Have systems to stay on track during crisis situations

The person you were *before* you read this book probably would have told you that this five-week program was too much work, and you'd never find time to do it—so maybe put the book aside and circle back to it . . . next week? Next month? In a year or so when things finally calm down? If you learned nothing else from our time together, I hope you've at least realized that when you put off important or personally significant tasks until some hypothetical future time, you're selling yourself short. Because over these past weeks, you put in the work and made the effort to start getting things done. You identi-fied the techniques and strategies that work best for you to help you deal with your procrastination and start work-ing toward the life you want. Your success and fulfillment should never be deferred to the future, because you can have them right now—today.

REFERENCES

Bernstein, Ethan S., and Stephen Turban. "The Impact of the 'Open' Workspace on Human Collaboration." *Philosophical Transactions of the Royal Society B*. 373, no. 1753 (July 2018). doi:10.1098 /rstb.2017.0239.

Case Western Reserve University. "Mindfulness in the Workplace Improves Employee Focus, Attention, Behavior, New Management-Based Research Concludes." *ScienceDaily*. March 10, 2016. Accessed October 29, 2018. www.sciencedaily.com/releases/2016/03 /160310141455.htm.

Davis, Daphne M., and Jeffrey A. Hayes. "What Are the Benefits of Mindfulness." *Monitor on Psychology* 43, no. 7 (July/August 2012): 64. www.apa.org/monitor/2012/07-08/ce-corner.aspx.

Denis, Katie. "Your Boss Wants You to Take a Vacation." *CNN*. Updated May 9, 2018. Accessed October 29, 2018. www.cnn .com/2018/05/09/opinions/take-more-vacation-days-america -opinion-denis/index.html.

Frontiers. "Serious Health Risks Associated with Energy Drinks." *ScienceDaily*. November 15, 2017. Accessed October 29, 2018. www.sciencedaily.com/releases/2017/11/171115124519.htm.

Godman, Heidi. "Regular Exercise Changes the Brain to Improve Memory, Thinking Skills." *Harvard Health Blog*. Updated April 5, 2018. www.health.harvard.edu/blog/regular-exercise-changes-brain -improve-memory-thinking-skills-201404097110.

Hamilton, Jon. "Think You're Multitasking? Think Again." *NPR*. October 2, 2008. Accessed October 29, 2018. www.npr.org/templates/story /story.php?storyId=95256794.

Harvard Health Publishing. "Blue Light Has a Dark Side." Harvard Health Letter. Updated August 13, 2018. Accessed October 29, 2018. www.health.harvard.edu/staying-healthy/blue-light-has-a-dark-side.

Mann, Denise. "Alcohol and a Good Night's Sleep Don't Mix." WebMD. January 22, 2013. Accessed October 29, 2018. www.webmd.com/sleep-disorders/news/20130118/alcohol-sleep#1.

Olson, Eric J. "How Many Hours of Sleep Are Enough for Good Health?" MayoClinic. Accessed October 29, 2018. www.mayoclinic.org/healthy-lifestyle/adult-health/expert-answers/how-many-hours-of-sleep-are-enough/faq-20057898.

Pattison, Kermit. "Worker, Interrupted: The Cost of Task Switching." *Fast Company*. July 28, 2018. Accessed October 29, 2018. www.fastcompany.com/944128/worker-interrupted-cost-task-switching.

Swaminathan, Nikhil. "Why Does the Brain Need So Much Power?" *Scientific American*. April 29, 2008. Accessed October 29, 2018. www.scientificamerican.com/article/why-does-the-brain-need-s.

Uncapher, M. R., M. K. Thieu, and A. D. Wagner. "Media Multitasking and Memory: Differences in Working Memory and Long-Term Memory." *Psychonomic Bulletin & Review* 23, no. 2 (April 2016): 483–90. doi:10.3758/s13423-015-0907-3.

Wenner, Melinda. "Smile! It Could Make You Happier: Making an Emotional Face—or Suppressing One—Influences Your Feelings." *Scientific American*. September 1, 2009. Accessed October 29, 2018. www.scientificamerican.com/article/smile-it-could-make-you-happier.

INDEX

ABOUT THE AUTHOR

 **Garland Coulson**, known as "Captain Time," is a popular speaker who has been teaching productivity and time management for more than 20 years. A simple gift from his manager of a Day-Timer more than 30 years ago started him on a lifelong quest to master productivity. As he learned how to become more personally productive, he found himself helping others who were also struggling with productivity.

Coulson's focus is on teaching people how to be more productive in a shorter amount of time so that they have more time for family, friends, passions, and those moments that take one's breath away. He lives with his wife, Terry Mack, in Spruce Grove, Alberta. You can follow him at CaptainTime.com and on YouTube: Youtube.com/c/GarlandCoulson.

CPSIA information can be obtained
at www.ICGtesting.com
Printed in the USA
LVHW020902230119
604815LV00001B/1/P